LIFE'S
TOO
F***ING
SHORT

A guide to getting what you
want out of life without
wasting time, effort, or money

JANET STREET-PORTER

CELESTIAL ARTS
BERKELEY

IN MEMORY OF DAINTON
Thanks to Peter, Neil, Emma, and all my long-suffering friends

Text copyright © 2008 by Janet Street-Porter
Illustrations copyright © 2008 by Quadrille Publishing, Ltd.

Published in the United States by Celestial Arts, an imprint of the Crown Publishing Group,
a division of Random House, Inc., New York.
www.crownpublishing.com
www.tenspeed.com

Celestial Arts and the Celestial Arts colophon are registered trademarks of Random House, Inc.

Library of Congress Cataloging-in-Publication Data
Street-Porter, Janet, 1946-
   Life's too f***ing short : a guide to getting what you want out of life without wasting time,
effort, or money / Janet Street-Porter.
   p. cm.
   ISBN-10: 1-58761-352-2 (alk. paper)
   ISBN-13: 978-1-58761-352-4 (alk. paper)
   1. Women—Conduct of life—Humor. I. Title. II. Title: Life's too fucking short.
   PN6231.C6142S77 2009b
   828'.9207—dc22
                    2009012070

ISBN: 978-1-58761-352-4

Originally published in Great Britain by Quadrille Publishing, Ltd., in 2008
Editorial Director: Anne Furniss
Creative Director: Helen Lewis
Editor: Jenni Muir
Photo research/Digital work: Paul Babb
Original Phootgraphy: Paul and Anne Babb, Janet Street-Porter
Illustrations: Bridget Bodoano
Exercises: Johnathan Parker personal training: jp©cafitness.co.uk
Production: Bridget Fish, Vincent Smith

Cover design by Katy Brown
Front cover photo © Getty Images
Back cover photo © ITV plc. Photo by Mike Lawn

Printed and bound in China

1 2 3 4 5 6 7 8 9 10—13 12 11 10 9

First U.S. Edition

LIFE'S TOO F***ING SHORT...

LIFE'S TOO F***ING SHORT to get depressed about being

* FORTY-SOMETHING
* FRIENDLESS * BROKE

I am a great believer in the power of positive thinking, and not expecting that life will be "lucky." How I hate that word, especially when people come up to me and say "you've had some lucky breaks in your career." No, I didn't. We are rewarded for working twice as hard as men to get noticed, for juggling all the competing bits of our lives. If we get a better job or a pay raise, it's because for it.

There's no point in getting bitter and twisted about this—that's the way it is. And don't bother picking up a magazine and feeling that everything in your life doesn't seem as interesting as what's going on in celebrity world. Be honest, do you want to be photographed every time you take out the trash or go to get a newspaper? Do you want to be telling journalists about how you've spent a load of money having your nose rebuilt? How your best friends are a bunch of gay men, your plumber is Ukrainian, and how you're never going to have kids? Too much information! Some celebrities are truly addicted to fame and feel that they have to include us—the public—in everything they think and do. Or they moan about a "lack of privacy" while beaming down at us from every billboard endorsing everything from eyeliner to handbags, getting paid two million dollars a deal.

Since I appeared on a reality TV show in Britain, people recognize me everywhere I go. It's fine—I couldn't care less. I was well paid and raised a lot of money for charity. I'm not going to moan on about people checking out my basket in supermarkets (I buy toilet rolls because I crap like normal people), or complain because someone calls out my name at an airport. I don't even get pissed off with workmen in white vans imitating my accent—because, at the end of the day they are sad, paunchy chaps sitting in white vans, and I am being driven around in a taxi paid for by a film company and I live in a nice house. If they were any good at impersonations I presume they would be on TV or the radio, and not mending pipes or delivering boxes all day.

I can write this book because I grew up weird looking, with big frilly teeth, thick glasses, and boring hair. I was the girl who never had a boyfriend at school, the last one in the class to wear a bra, the girl others used to call "lezzie" in the changing rooms for netball. Externally I might have seemed gauche and insecure, but inside I knew I was special and different. I've always had a huge amount of self-belief. Sure, it was tempered with a healthy dollop of insecurity brought about by my looks and my strong accent, and the fact that from the moment I was on the radio and then on television the critics loved to try and criticize me as much as possible. But instead of letting it get me down, I just got stronger.

DECODE THE TWADDLE
BEAMED AT YOU EVERY DAY

We are assaulted with advice on every side, from fashion and beauty writers to "tips" from celebrities. Newspapers and magazines now give a large amount of space, not just to advice columnists, but also to "life" gurus, and advisers who lecture us on everything from diet to ethical living. The end result, after reading the Saturday or Sunday papers, with all their supplements, is utter exhaustion and a sense of confusion and inadequacy.

A huge industry has grown up that purports to "help" women, but in my opinion just does the complete opposite.

How many times have you found a little stack of scraps of newsprint, perhaps "useful" addresses culled from magazines, pushed under the phone book or a vase? Honestly, you could spend hours every week online— making friends, ordering organic food, checking out designer fashion. You could spend half a day a week (and a considerable sum of money) on the latest beauty treatments, trying to stave off the inevitable aging process. You could cross the country sourcing organic, hand-reared ingredients to make perfect suppers. OR YOU COULD HAVE A LIFE. I am trying to wean myself off this addiction— hoarding cuttings that list who does the "ultimate facial," where to buy the "best handmade pasta," or where to source "jeans that flatter every figure."

ADOPT A HEALTHY CYNICISM ABOUT SO-CALLED EXPERTS

Once experts had qualifications and certificates, but now they are self-appointed gurus who specialize in everything from reading the irises of our eyes to the state of our large intestines. You can call up parenting experts, eco-auditors, feng shui experts, wardrobe advisers, and people who come around and de-clutter your home, chucking stuff in trash bags. I feel weak just reading about this army of experts who can (for a hefty fee) sort out my life and hopefully make me feel calmer and less stressed. But it's all twaddle of course . . . .

I was reading an article the other day, entitled "How To Be Happy." Apparently there is an equation that defines this: $H=S+C+V$, where H=Happiness, S is the biological point at which you feel happy, C is the conditions of your life, and V the voluntary choices you make. Confused? I certainly was. Especially when the writer went on to talk about the perfect conditions to produce happiness, defining them as Peace and Quiet, Relationships, and Sharing. TALK ABOUT STATING THE BLOODY OBVIOUS. Of course it is important to have some reflective time in your life, but the right sounds (like music) can make you happy, ecstatic and uplifted. Relationships—obviously a good relationship is ideal, but do you know anyone who would ever define their most important relationship as anything other than difficult? Let's be realistic, the best thing about relationships is not to let them dominate your life or penetrate your inner psyche. Sharing—well, that goes without saying, but there's a fine line between sharing and being drained. At the end of reading this "expert" view I was more than a bit cross that I'd wasted ten minutes trying to understand a theory that seemed full of holes. In the end, we can all be as happy or as miserable as we want—if we feel miserable, only we can resolve that, not an expert, not a bloke, not a pill, not an alternative treatment, and definitely not a face cream.

Talking of treatments, I read about one the other day in which you put yourself in a compartment chilled to minus 211 degrees—that's six times colder than a domestic freezer! This is cryotherapy, and its advocates claim that it stimulates all our bodily functions, improving circulation and our immune response. The writer said it improves skin quality, "clearing away lactic acid and toxins." **STOP RIGHT THERE!** A "holistic" doctor claimed "it is as though our healing response has become dormant only to be reawakened instantly." A British Medical Association (BMA) spokesman told the writer "it is not inconceivable that reduced temperatures might have quite substantial side effects."

WHEN YOU ANALYZE THE TWADDLE THAT PASSES FOR INFORMED COPY IN WOMEN'S MAGAZINES THESE DAYS, YOU FIND GLARING HOLES.

The BMA bloke used the word "might." And he didn't use the word "benefits" as a byproduct of the treatment, but used the far more cautious term "side effects." The journalist claimed that she felt "elated" after her three-minute session, which cost a whopping $60. I am sure that a lot of alternative therapies, like massage and acupuncture, do give huge benefits— but they don't work for everyone. What I thoroughly object to is the presentation of this stuff as if it were unassailable truth, when, in fact, it often just fills up space under the guise of telling us about the latest must-have treatment.

We are being offered more kinds of beauty products, more kinds of therapies like this than ever. The net result of all this choice? Three quarters of all women in their thirties and forties say they are lucky to get six hours of sleep a night and many say they feel tired all the time. A survey found that a whopping fifty-nine percent of women over thirty said they felt tired "all the time," and only one in twelve ate a proper breakfast, getting through the day eating snacks rather than meals. Now an increasing number of women get headaches, eczema, chest infections, and heart palpitations—all manifestations of the stressed lives they lead.

Life's too short for all of this.

SOMEHOW WE MUST IMPROVE OUR QUALITY OF LIFE, BUT **IT IS UP TO US** TO PRIORITIZE, STOP DOING SOME THINGS AND FIND TIME FOR OURSELVES.

The current situation is a sad reflection of our attempts to have it all, and in the end our health suffers. You can chuck money at quick-fix solutions like beauty treatments, but in truth, you need to have a radical rethink.

THE MOST IMPORTANT PERSON IN YOUR LIFE— THE PERSON WHO SETS THE RULES, DECIDES THE AGENDA, CHUCKS OUT THE MENTAL AND PHYSICAL DETRITUS—**IS YOU.**

WHEN YOU WAKE UP,
LIE STILL FOR TWO MINUTES

Recite over and over again:

I AM BLOODY BRILLIANT.

I AM GREAT.

I AM NUMBER ONE.

UNIQUE.

I LIKE ME.

I AM WORTH IT.

I AM HIGHLY INTELLIGENT,
NO MATTER WHAT OTHERS MAY SAY.

You have to do this, because, take it from me, no one else is ever going to tell you that in the coming twenty-four hours. To value myself is the single most important thing I have learned over the years. No one ever did me a favor. No one ever gave me a career break out of pity. I did it all for myself. By believing in myself.

SET AN AGENDA,
AND WRITE A SHORT LIST
BEFORE YOU GO TO BED
EVERY NIGHT

Do not put more than five or six things on it—any more would be unrealistic. On a day-to-day basis, don't make lists you can't achieve. You should not carry over more than a couple of things to the next day's list. At the same time, stop and spend a few hours alone, making a plan for yourself.

DECIDE WHAT YOU ARE NOT GOING TO DO ANY MORE

* the people you are not going to call back ✔
* the books you will never read ✔
* the relatives you can send to social Siberia ✔
* the food you are not going to cook ✔
* the man/men you're not going to wait on hand and foot any more ✔
* the clothes you will not buy ✔
* the stuff you don't need ✔
* the boring job you're not going to suffer any longer ✔

Plan your time to make sure that every week you set aside a slot for stuff that you want to do—grow lettuces on the windowsill, go to evening classes, join a walking club, learn another language, plan an activity vacation with people you don't know. Hopefully this book will give you a starting point. Establish your own rules and stick to them. Good luck!

unpromising raw material!

LIFE'S TOO F***ING SHORT TO SPEND $200 ON FACE CREAM

thin me 1997 never achieved since

- Ignore beauty journalists
- Make the most of what you've got
- How to find a great hairdresser

Why do intelligent women have shelves of rotting makeup⁉

Why are so-called beauty writers lying cows⁉
Why is most expensive face cream a waste of money⁉
Why is there so much pressure to have cosmetic surgery⁉
Why bother to read "top tips" coming from the famous⁉

IT'S WHY-OH-WHY TIME

IF THE BEAUTY INDUSTRY HAD TO GO THROUGH THE KIND OF CHECKS IMPOSED ON THE CARS WE DRIVE OR THE FOOD WE EAT, IT WOULD GO OUT OF BUSINESS.

Has there ever been such a massive industry built entirely on wishful thinking? Just as nine women out of ten aren't happy with the shape of their bodies, four out of five of us think that in a laboratory somewhere a miracle worker of a scientist is going to come up with a cream that will stop the aging process, iron out wrinkles, tighten up flabby chins, and take a decade off our appearances if we slavishly slather it on day in and day out. **THERE IS NO SUCH CREAM AND PROBABLY NEVER WILL BE.** While there may be a raft of rules and regulations ensuring that the products we put on our skin do not actually harm us, there is nothing to ensure that they will actually deliver what they promise. The food industry is strictly regulated, and recently a major margarine was ordered to alter their advertising so that they could only claim that their spreads lowered your cholesterol as *part* of a healthy regime involving diet and exercise. No such tight controls seem to operate when it comes to the ludicrous claims we read in ads for face cream, anticellulite gel, and skin-brightening products.

From the age of eleven I worshipped at the altar of self-improvement.

Didn't we all? Given the raw material of my genetic inheritance it wasn't surprising that I looked in the mirror and felt miserable. I had big, sticky-out teeth, National Health glasses like milk-bottle bottoms, long legs like sticks, a completely flat chest, and beige hair. Hair that lay flat on my head and wasn't the slightest bit interested in being wavy, curly, or interesting.

When I was smaller my mother would tear up strips of old sheets and tie my hair in rags, night after night. Soon I suffered from acute sleep deprivation—it was like sleeping on a bag of marbles. Every morning Mum would unwrap these tight twirls of cotton, and hey presto—my hair sank limply onto my head, straight but with a weird kink halfway down.

By the time I was fourteen I was determined to go blonde in the name of glamour, but dyed hair was forbidden at school. In desperation, I noticed that new brands of toothpaste were emblazoned "with added peroxide," and so I would sit in class, TOOTHPASTE TUBE IN HAND hidden under the desk, METHODICALLY RUBBING COLGATE INTO MY HAIR for hours at a time. After a few weeks it resembled a set of matted dreadlocks, but when I washed off the accumulated gunk, I was left with the same flat, boring beige hair I'd had before I started. It was a sad day!

Next, I bought a spray to dye my hair silver and used that whenever I went out clubbing. It was fine, so long as no one actually touched my head, as it came right off.

I tried false fingernails and was embarrassed when dancing with a cute boy and they dropped off, like nasty bird talons, in his hand. I got fabulous false eyelashes, but I didn't glue them on very carefully and they would eventually start to come off and droop over my eyes like sagging venetian blinds. Once I shagged a well-known artist after he'd given a lecture at Cambridge University—in the morning I found my false eyelashes lying on the sheets, like a couple of dead furry caterpillars. I prayed that he hadn't seen them.

Over the years I changed my glasses and my hair more than most people change their underwear. The results were generally horrible, and when I am on my deathbed I intend to summon all the shit hairdressers I have paid over the years and read them the riot act. I have had pink hair, orange hair, black and white extensions, a yellow star dyed in my hair, and dreary blonde streaks. It's been bobbed, cropped, and left to fester for two years, long and lank.

Why oh why does it take twenty years of failures to find a haircut that works?

Here's my advice: forget everything you read about fashionable hairstyles, there's only ever going to be one that works on your head anyway. Why I grew my hair long I do not know, because I have no idea how to put it up or style it in any way. It was probably because I couldn't face telling my hairdresser that I didn't like the way he cut my hair, but because he was so nice I couldn't face sacking him! I spent two years walking around with my hair up in a clip because it was hot and heavy. Loads and loads of women have exactly the same relationship with their hairdressers—sick isn't it? Hair is such a barometer of your inner turmoil, and when you go to the hairdresser, and they start to snip at your bangs, don't you just start to panic? It's as if you've been caught out shopping without any underwear on—most of us use our hair as a versatile way of hiding at least a third of our faces. Short bangs make you feel naked. Hairdressing salons are places of utter misery.

LIFE'S TOO SHORT TO HAVE YOUR HAIR DONE BY SOMEONE WHO HASN'T A CLUE.

Don't you just know as they start to blow-dry, that it's all going to come out wrong? My palms start sweating, and before long I start to feel queasy. I have walked out of more hairdressers with wet hair than I want to remember. The thing is, they are practicing on you—they are not the people who have to go home and live with the result. Mostly, they couldn't give a flying f***, and the best you can hope for is ten percent of their concentration. They are generally bored, and you aren't interesting or famous enough to engage them. If I go to a salon where I have never been before, I always ask the youngest stylist to blow-dry my hair—at least they'll have their finger on the pulse of what's happening, as opposed to some bitter old senior stylist.

THE PHOTOS OF ME OVER THE YEARS ARE LIVING PROOF THAT A HAIRDRESSER CAN BE A WOMAN'S WORST ENEMY.

I'm tall, so why would I want really short hair unless I am as skinny as a top model? Unless you are a size ten, once you pass thirty, and are taller than average, just forget getting your hair cropped, no matter what your hairdresser claims. You will just look like a scout mistress or a clothes pin.

Let's talk about that stuff hairdressers call "products." What is this gunk they slather on? It's called things like MUD, LIFT, ANTI-FRIZZ, RELAXANT, VOLUME CONTROL—all totally mystifying. I culled the following product names from a recent magazine feature about stuff that claims to make your hair shine more: LAMINATE WEIGHTLESS SHINE..... VOLUMIZING POLISH..... POLISHING MILK..... COLOR SHINE

IT'S GOBBLEDEGOOK

BRIGHTENER LOTION... PROFESSIONAL LUMINOUS MASK... ANTIAGING POLISHING SERUM.... ILLUMINATING SHAMPOO.

Confused? We've got serums, gels, masks, milk, shampoo, and polish— which all proves that very few hairdressers excelled in twelfth-grade English class. I guarantee that if your hairdresser puts loads of different "products" on your hair, you will never achieve the same look at home. And if the end result in the salon involves complicated blow-drying or—my idea of complete hell—the use of rollers, forget it.

Hairdressers talk a whole load of rubbish about what they are slapping on your hair— it's all designed to get you back through their door on a weekly basis.

By the way, the reason why my hair always looks really shiny—it's dyed! God knows what horrible gray color exists under the bucket of red vegetable coloring that gets dumped on it every three weeks. I certainly am not interested in the natural look, nor should any woman be over the age of forty! So how do you get great hair?

Life's too short to visit the

PURE AND SIMPLE.

hairdresser every seven days—are you made of money?

I have to have hair that looks good for filming and television work. It has taken me **THIRTY YEARS** to find a nice, nonegotistical hairdresser who comes around to my house on his scooter, cuts, dyes, and blow-dries my hair in record time. Whatever he costs is cheaper and less stressful than schlepping to a salon on the other side of London, buying cups of coffee, being charged for a glass of water, and listening to some skinny bitch in the chair next to you moaning about her housekeeper, her boyfriend, her nanny. Now I have hair that looks the same week in and week out—perfect! It's cut so that I can wash it, rub my head with a towel, and it comes out approximately the same. Try to get a hairdresser you know and trust to come around to your home or office after work, and get a couple of friends to combine their appointments with yours. That way the stylist can make a decent amount of money, and you can all sit around having something to eat and a drink. That way, getting your hair done is fun. And here's my ultimate tip: **LIFE'S TOO SHORT TO WASH YOUR HAIR MORE THAN ONCE A WEEK.** When I appeared on a reality show in the Australian jungle, my hairdresser gave me an excellent piece of advice: don't wash your hair. For three weeks all I ever did was splash it with cold water in order to damp down the smell of the fire I did the cooking on. Hair cleans itself, and after a limp couple of days it sorts itself out and actually feels thicker and has more body. It didn't go frizzy, the color didn't fade in the sun—in short, it looked far better than I did wearing horrible baggy shorts and a red fleece with "JSP" and a phone number emblazoned across my back. When I go on vacation, or when I'm traveling and not filming or doing television, I only wash my hair once a week at the most. And I never, ever wash it more than once. I use the minimum amount of shampoo and never use conditioner. You need to cut right back on the crap you use. It all piles up and makes hair lank, and doesn't allow it to sort itself out naturally. The only reason I wash my hair more often is if I've been in a room or club with smokers—but as they are banned from more or less everywhere now, that is relatively rare. And, after filming in an abattoir for the TV show *The F-Word* on a couple of occasions—the smell of freshly slaughtered carcasses sticks to absolutely everything—I had to wash my hair and everything I was wearing, too.

LIFE'S TOO SHORT TO SPEND A FORTUNE ON FACE CREAM.

I am sixty, and I might be a bit lumpy around the midriff, but I have great skin—it's one of the few things I can sincerely thank my late mother for. I have small wrinkles around my eyes, bags under them after a late night, and a saggy chin, but who has time to notice these minor deficiencies? Every day of my life someone compliments me on my skin and says I don't look my age. Well, I do look my age if I feel miserable, am sulking or falling asleep, believe me!

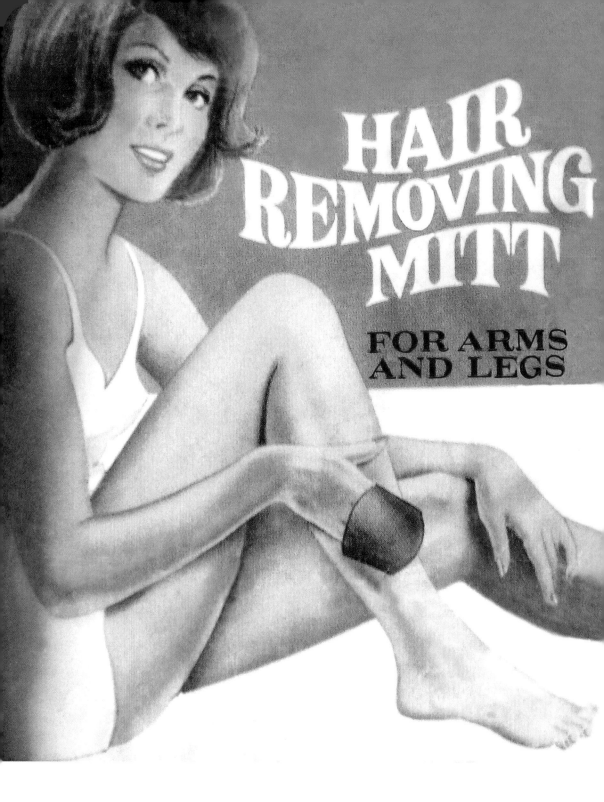

Women often ask what is the secret of good skin—apart from genetics—and it is simple, but so hard to achieve:

* not smoking
* refusing illegal drugs
* drinking loads of water
* sleeping at least six hours a night
* wearing sun block
* enjoying life (miseries do look wrinkly, don't they?)

I look at the Duchess of Cornwall, younger than me, with horrible pleats all around her mouth from puffing on dozens of cigarettes a day for decades. Even if she's given up now to please Charles, it's too late, the damage has been done. Ditto sunbathing. Luckily I wore glasses all the time until I was in my fifties, which protected the skin around my eyes from wind. I also wore sunglasses in bright light to avoid screwing my eyes up too much, still do. Now that I have had my eyes lasered they are more exposed. I haven't got glasses to hide behind, but my wrinkles are relatively fine.

It doesn't matter what crap is written on the tube of eye cream, once you've got wrinkles they are not going to go away.

What do you want the cream to do—turn into thread and make a giant pleat in your face? I have facials every couple of months but, quite honestly, it's more about lying down, being pampered, and having my eyebrows and facial hair dealt with than about any radical improvement on my appearance. Facials aren't going to change your skin overnight. But beauticians (who are generally ordinary working girls and not overpaid beauty writers who get loads of freebies) do give out some top tips. One told me to alternate cheap face cream with expensive gunk, as our skin gets used to any kind of cream. I use products from the supermarket that cost no more than $20—and I guarantee I get the same results as I would with moisturizers that cost $160 and more a pot.

THE TRICK WITH SKIN CARE IS TO KEEP IT VERY SIMPLE. **GET UP,** WASH YOUR FACE WITH CREAM OR CLEANSER, EVERY SINGLE DAY **(I HAVE NEVER USED SOAP ON MY FACE SINCE I WAS FOURTEEN).** PUT ON MOISTURIZER. PUT SOME CREAM OR GEL AROUND YOUR EYES. **THAT'S IT.**

Every night I cleanse my face even if I am so drunk I can't talk.

I slap on moisturizer and eye cream, then hit the pillow. That is the sum total of my so-called beauty regime. If ever I am tempted to use some of the antiaging crap I'm sent, I can guarantee you that within a week the area around my eyes starts to go red, my skin begins to itch and feel oversensitive. On the odd occasion that I have let a beauty therapist scour my skin (or exfoliate, as they call it), it was sore the next day. Facials bring out blemishes you never knew you had.

I never wear foundation or heavy makeup, just tinted moisturizer. **POWDER IS TOTALLY AGING IF YOU ARE OVER FORTY.** I wear eye makeup, pencil and shadow (mascara and liner if I'm working or at a party), and lipstick. Takes five minutes. **TOO MUCH CRAP ON YOUR SKIN WILL RUIN IT.** If a makeup artist puts base on my face because it looks washed out in the bright lights of a television studio, I remove it the minute I leave the studio.

Such a lot of drivel is written about "hydrating" your skin. You cannot put water back into your skin no matter what you might read. All creams do is enable your skin to feel softer and more oily, not wetter. They can contain sun block, which is good, too. But no one wants to make it sound that basic, do they? One beauty writer wrote the other day about a problem I must admit I had never thought of for one nanosecond of my sixty years: "aging metal that lurks in your skin." She went on to say: "chelating agents such as lactobionic acid and gluconolactone (both new PHAs) are said to capture free iron in upper skin layers and reduce its oxidizing, and therefore aging, potential." If you can understand that DRIVEL then you must be a top scientist. The key lies in the inclusion of the words "are said to," which means, in a nutshell, that the manufacturers of the creams she's talking about, i.e., plugging (which cost $68 and $200 a pot), have made these claims, and she doesn't know whether or not there is any real scientific evidence to support a dotty theory that metal is lurking in our skin and needs to be removed with expensive cream. And does anyone outside the rarefied corridors of beauty magazines actually commonly use the word "chelation"—which means, according to my dictionary, the treatment of heavy-metal (i.e., lead) poisoning?

HOW NOT TO HAVE BAGS UNDER YOUR EYES.

Feeling particularly tired one day, I made an appointment with a top cosmetic surgeon who specialized in removing the bags under your eyes by making an incision that would hardly be seen. He took one look at me and told me I needed a full face-lift as well to deal with my sagging chin. It cost $1,500 for that consultation and the basic operation for my bags would have cost $14,000. I felt repulsive after thirty minutes of talking to this patronizing man. A month later, I went on vacation, didn't take my computer, stopped drinking half a bottle of wine a day, and slept properly. The bags under my eyes reduced by half immediately, and I spent the $14,000 I had saved on having my garden landscaped. Hoorah! Once you go down the Botox route there's no turning back. The way I look at it, a lot of cosmetic surgery is more to do with psychological problems and general insecurities than anything else. The surgical removal of the bags under my eyes would not get me a better sex life, it would not get rid of my fat stomach, and it certainly wouldn't get me better, higher-paid work. And the chances are that within a couple of years I would need to have the operation done all over again.

Face-lifts have to be redone regularly, and soon you will start to look like a startled goldfish,

(like many expressionless, rich American women I know with no ear lobes and whose age can only really be determined by looking at the backs of their hands). Once you start injecting your face with Botox and fillers, then you have embarked upon a process that is highly addictive in itself. Too many women expect these procedures to give them benefits outside the purely visual. As for attending "Botox evenings"—forget it. Why bow to peer pressure? It is a tough decision to take, at a time when the price of cosmetic surgery and minor procedures is coming down, but deep down, I do think you have to accept the aging process and its effect on your face. A mobile, active face will always seem more youthful, and you can certainly do facial exercises if you think they will tighten your jaw line—just don't let anyone see you.

WE ARE BOMBARDED WITH UNREALISTIC IMAGES OF OTHER WOMEN AND THEREFORE FEEL WE DON'T MAKE THE GRADE.

On my desk is a page torn from the beauty section of a best-selling women's glossy magazine. The journalist is describing something called the "Ultimate Face-Lift Treatment," which costs a whopping $900 for the first appointment. Apparently this experience involves "a combination of bipolar radio frequency and optical energy (either laser or light)." So far we are in mumbo-jumbo land. Her face was zapped with these rays (I assume on a free treatment), a procedure which, according to her, "heats the dermal tissue to 131 degrees and stimulates collagen production, to tighten the skin." But how does she know? Five sessions are recommended—in other words a whopping $4,000!!! The photograph on this page is not of the journalist in question, but shows a moonlit beauty aged about eighteen, with alabaster-smooth skin, bathed in dew and tinted soft blue.

Get a grip, girls— airbrushing is commonplace in the world of beauty mythology and women's magazines. It is thoroughly evil. It just makes readers feel inferior and inadequate. This is unattainable perfection.

We all live real lives, with noisy kids, irritating partners, demanding jobs. We don't live in an airbrushed world, and it is always a shock to meet anyone very famous, because you see them as they really are, and not how some magazine editor would like to project them. From Elle Macpherson to Kelly Osbourne to Kate Winslet to Sienna Miller—all look normal, albeit very attractive, in the flesh—and, to be fair, all have said that they don't like being altered in this way. Look at the cover of any women's magazine—the face gazing out at you will have been doctored by an airbrush technician, removing wrinkles and sags better than any cream could ever do. And yet the result is presented to us as reality, something that we should aspire to. It makes me feel physically ill, and is causing a whole generation of young women to grow up with a warped idea of what their bodies and their faces should look like. Recently, two makeup companies have been found guilty of manipulating the truth about mascara—using fake eyelashes and airbrushing in their adverts. You'd never get the same look by just slathering on their products.

Beauty editors—how do they sleep at night? Traitors to their sex, the lot of them!

LIFE'S TOO F***ING SHORT TO TRY TO BE A SIZE ZERO

- How to eat so you are in control of your body
- How to exercise without realizing it
- How to achieve a body image that is realistic

I promise you that diets never work in the long term. There is plenty of evidence demonstrating conclusively that most fatties go back to being fatties in the long run, even if they embark on a diet and initially lose a large amount of weight. Gradually our bodies learn to adapt and our metabolism will override any restricted eating plans that have been foisted on it. All those pounds you crash-dieted off in the beginning will gradually go back on, until you end up just five or six pounds lighter than when you were at your fattest. Believe me, I've been there. The trick is not to let your weight gradually accumulate in the first place, because getting rid of it is increasingly difficult as you get older. Our body shapes are determined by genetics, and it is only possible to alter them within a small range.

The tough fact is that you cannot fundamentally change your body shape unless you do one of two things. The most radical solution is to spend a lot of money and opt for cosmetic surgery, and the truth is that relying on liposuction to remove fat is no long-term solution as it will just go back on in a couple of years and you'll have to have the same operation—which is major surgery—all over again. Do we really want our bodies to be scarred and dimpled where all those fries and donuts have been siphoned out?

Secondly, you can adopt the same mindset as Madonna. This woman ruthlessly exercises and works out and watches everything she eats in order to maintain a toned physique and cheat the aging process. She looks amazing for someone who has recently turned fifty and has had a couple of kids. The only giveaway is her hands. She might have regular facials and probably has had subtle noninvasive tightening around her chin, but if you want to know how she's really aging, look at the backs of her hands. Now her arms are starting to look stringy from years of lifting weights and those punishing routines in the gym. Do you think that Madonna looks like a woman who is having a lot of fun? No she doesn't. She's working in the entertainment business where she's competing with rising young female stars in their twenties. She's a perfectionist, determined to present the best image possible at all times. Madonna doesn't really do casual. I've met her a few times and we've had dinner—she's highly intelligent, but lacking in humor. She doesn't really inhabit our world, with mess, food binges, and the odd bottle of wine too many. She's organized, focused, disciplined. That's why she's worth hundreds of millions of dollars and we're not. But, let's be honest—isn't it a hell of a lot more fun to sit in a bar with a girlfriend downing a bottle of Sauvignon Blanc, laughing and joking, and eating a steak? Or would you rather be drinking a bowl of miso soup and chewing each mouthful of steamed fish fifty times in pursuit of the perfect ass?

Life's too short to start every day with three grapefruit segments, a cup of black coffee, and a couple of nuts.

THE KEY TO OUR RELATIONSHIP WITH FOOD AND ITS IMPACT ON OUR BODIES IS MODERATION AND REALISM ABOUT WHAT IS ACHIEVABLE.

I have been to health farms (or spas as they are now known) many times. I've been away to group events where I gave up booze, did yoga, and sat through lectures on how to concoct slimming salad dressings. I've detoxed. I've had colonic irrigation. I've sweated in Turkish baths and saunas. I've had sadistic beauticians wrap me in freezing gel and slather me with boiling volcanic mud in the hope of slenderizing my thighs. I have religiously read every diet printed in a national newspaper over the last two decades.

I HAVE STARVED MYSELF OVER A WEEKEND, given up tea, coffee, sugar, salt, carbs, wheat, and dairy, all at different times and in different combinations.

WHAT THE HELL FOR? WHAT F***ING MYTHICAL SLENDER VERSION OF JSP WAS I DREAMING OF MORPHING INTO?

I have paid hundreds of dollars to dieticians and nutritionists who've ordered me to spend even more money on bottles of special oils and potions. They've made me put drops of various tinctures in water before every meal. They've drawn ludicrous charts itemizing foods I could eat and those I should avoid. They've listed "good" and "bad" fruits and vegetables. All that happened after a month of these complicated regimes was that I farted all the time and became incredibly constipated.

Over time I have come to the gradual conclusion that the only way to stay at the right (and by that I mean healthy) weight is to eat three times a day, never miss a meal, and eat as slowly as you possibly can. You can adopt a different eating plan every single week if you want, **BUT THE PLAIN TRUTH OF THE MATTER IS, CRANKY DIETS DON'T WORK.**

They are a total waste of time.

Most women (and plenty of men) feel bombarded with images of a physical perfection they feel they have to emulate. Why? Most of the models in glossy magazines are teenagers who could never possibly afford or want to wear the expensive clothes fashion editors have put them in for the photographic session. Most models smoke. They do not eat more than one mini-meal a day. They look obscenely skinny and weird in real life. Many famous women who are constantly photographed by the paparazzi spend so much time throwing up after eating a few prawns and a dozen leaves of

SUNDAY

BREAKFAST
Grapefruit
Black coffee

LUNCH
Any appetizer
Any meat
Any vegetable
One-half helping
dessert

DINNER
Scrambled eggs
Sliced tomatoes

MONDAY

BREAKFAST
Grapefruit
Black coffee

LUNCH
Chicken sandwich
on rye toast
(no butter)
Raw tomatoes

DINNER
Stalk of celery
Steak, good-sized helping
Tomato and
endive
salad
on lettuce
(no dressing)
Half grapefruit

TUESDAY

BREAKFAST
Grapefruit
Black coffee

LUNCH
Scrambled eggs
Sliced tomatoes
Apple

DINNER
Broiled halibut
Green salad
Celery and olives
Any vegetable
Sliced oranges

WED

LUNCH
Minute steak
Stewed tomat

wild arugula that they have developed a thick layer of unattractive fur. They have no body fat left after years of dieting and vomiting, and their metabolisms are totally f***ed. Their poor, wrecked bodies are growing the fur in order to try and keep warm. Believe me, I've sat and dined with these women, I've shared a bottle of wine with them at extremely close quarters. This is the horrible truth: FURRY ARMS. A famous footballer's wife has them. A couple of millionairess models have them. So does a stick-thin television presenter. Close up, these women's arms are covered with a thick down—it's the real giveaway of the damage they have done to themselves in order to get into a dress that would fit a normal eight-year-old. Their heads look too big for their bodies. They have no fat at the back of their shoulders. It is repulsive beyond belief.

The hardest lesson in life to learn is to accept the limitations of your own body. Until I was forty I was extremely thin for my height, just like my mum and dad. I took up jogging in the 1980s but gave it up after I slipped a disk twice. Then I made several television series where I walked extremely long distances, day in and day out. For one I climbed all the mountain ranges in Wales and traveled over 300 miles. The end result: my hips don't need replacing, but I've had several operations to clean out the joints. I have exercised regularly for the last twenty years, and it is only in the last two years, when I've been plagued with minor injuries in my hips and shoulder, that I've put on weight. I'd like to lose it, but it's not going to be achievable beyond a few pounds because I lead a busy life, and I do not believe in starvation.

PLEASE DO NOT AIM TO REDUCE YOUR WEIGHT BY MORE THAN ONE DRESS SIZE.

Men cannot understand why women want to be as thin as Victoria Beckham. They think she looks ridiculous. Men like women who have curves. They don't understand our obsession with having a flat stomach. Historically women never have had flat stomachs without wearing a corset. We will never achieve it by dieting, only by starvation.

Life's too short to spend half an hour every f***ing morning doing sit-ups. Learn how to emphasize the good bits of your body and camouflage the wobbly bits.

The exercises I do are to maintain fitness and flexibility, not gain the body of an Olympic athlete or the stomach of a supermodel. Of course you want to feel energetic, and you want your arms and legs to be toned. But getting rid of a huge roll around your middle is going to be very difficult if it's been there for more than a couple of years. You can aim to shrink it— by regular exercise and eating differently—but you will never eliminate it.

REMEMBER THAT ALL BEAUTY EDITORS ARE IN THE PAY OF THE BUSINESS THEY PROMOTE. THEY GET FREE TRIPS TO SPAS AND PRETEND THESE PLACES WORK MIRACLES. **THEY DON'T. THEY TELL YOU ANTICELLULITE CREAM MAKES A DIFFERENCE. IT'S UTTER BILGE.**

A good body comes from within—it's a mental attitude. You can look great if you're a size 18, and could never get a size-8 frock over your head. If men hate stick women, why do so many of us seek to emulate them? You have to put yourself first, eating in a way that gives you enough energy to get on with your life, fills you up, and—most importantly of all—is both rewarding and enjoyable.

Don't demonize food.

You also have to set aside an hour of every day when you'll exercise—and I'll explain how shortly.

YOUR EATING PLAN ON THE NO-DIET DIET

Plan a whole week's eating before you go shopping. Only buy food once a week. I start every day the same way, by drinking a mug of hot water with a slice of lemon in it. I might even have a couple.

BREAKFAST: Monday to Friday I eat the same breakfast—fruit—a big bowl of strawberries, raspberries, pomegranate seeds, blueberries, chopped-up apples with a dollop of plain, nonfat yogurt.

If I am constipated, I mix in a couple of spoonfuls of a high-fiber cereal. I drink coffee, no milk, no sugar. In winter I eat porridge—it takes five minutes to make and fills me up for hours until lunch. I make it with no salt, no milk, just water, and sprinkle berries on top, not syrup, to sweeten it.

Saturday and Sunday I eat a "normal" breakfast—a scrambled egg, mushrooms, a slice of bacon. One piece of toast. It's my reward for the rest of the week's breakfasts.

LIFE'S TOO F***ING SHORT TO ABANDON A GREAT BREAKFAST.

LUNCH: If I am out, I buy a salad or make my own and carry it to work in a plastic box. I like a piece of cold chicken, salmon, or smoked trout, green leaves, a little oil and vinegar dressing, no bread. Or I have chickpeas or lentils (drained, out of a can) and spicy dressing. During the day I drink tea—no milk, no sugar.

DINNER: Red meat no more than two or three times a week, white meat, such as chicken, more often. Game (pheasant, partridge) is great, too, and grilled fish (remember oily fish is good for you). I only eat pasta once a week. I eat loads of vegetables, especially cabbage and broccoli, beans and peas. I love green vegetables. I try not to eat too much cheese. I hardly eat butter or cream.

THAT'S IT FOLKS. I'd like to be fourteen pounds lighter, but when you're over fifty dieting can make you look much older. If you're too thin, you get very wrinkly. I'd rather have a roll of flab around my middle than a load of droopy skin on my neck, and that's the stark choice I've had to make. Also, cooking and eating makes me as happy as having sex—and that's saying something.

Why deny something that

gives you pleasure—are you a masochist?

Every day of my life I am told I look great for my age. Truly, it is a question of mental attitude more than anything else. I've been thinner, and I've been miserable. **NEVER ADOPT AN EATING REGIME THAT MAKES YOU FEEL DISPIRITED AND LOW.**

Buying all the food you need for a week in one go can help you to stop binging. You can pick at leftovers when you are starving. Build in treats like dark chocolate, but make one bar last a week.

EATING OUT

Don't drink at lunchtime, and order two starters in the evening, instead of a starter and a main course. Never order dessert—you can pick at someone else's portion! Don't have your first drink of the day until 7 P.M. and avoid beer, mixers, spirits, and fizzy water. Stick to wine and, if you overdo it, spend a couple of days cutting your daily quota of wine in half. Ban potato chips—instead eat a few nuts or seeds or raw vegetables dipped in tahini or hummus. I make the waiter remove the basket of bread from the table, otherwise I would eat it. I try to drink a glass of water for every glass of wine.

RESTRICTING SALT AND SUGAR AND OTHER EVILS

When I did the reality show, the reason I took control of the cooking was to regulate portions, make sure everyone got enough to eat, and to make food tasty without using sugar or salt—we were given no seasonings at all. I used fruit peelings to make tea, turned the outer leaves of vegetables into stock. I didn't miss sugar because I don't eat it anyway. Your body has to be gradually re-educated not to crave these drugs. I stopped when I went on a long trek in the Himalayas twenty years ago. Since then I've drunk my tea and coffee black, without sugar. I stopped eating butter by just spreading a tiny amount of jam on a piece of toast and eating it. I stopped having milk with cereal by mashing ripe fruit into oats and nuts. **IT IS TOUGH AT FIRST, BUT GRADUALLY YOU CAN WEAN YOUR BODY OFF SWEET THINGS.** And dark chocolate that's eighty to eighty-five percent cocoa solids is far less sweet than any other kind.

In all of this, be flexible. If I am staying with friends, I don't inflict my regime on them, but adapt it. In hotels, I always pack some fruit in case they have a crap selection on offer. I always take my own cereal. I spend as little time as possible preparing food to eat during the day, but I make sure that I have sorted out a nonfattening, filling lunch and stashed it in a plastic container.

I never buy ready-made sauces. I keep cans of lentils, chickpeas, kidney beans, cranberry beans—they are all really good sources of fiber.
I eat a couple of sticks of celery every day when I get the munchies. My fridge is packed with vegetables and fruit. You have to create your own rewards. But you also have to limit spuds and bread and regard them as occasional treats. Mayonnaise is another occasional extra, not something you are going to drench every salad with.

YOUR DIET AND YOUR PARTNER

If losing weight and getting into shape is tough, it's even tougher when the person you live with isn't interested. The men in my life fall into two categories—the super-slobs and the manically fit. The slobs just ate even more when I got healthy and trim. One husband would lope off to the garage to smoke cigars, pretending he was washing the car. After a massive Sunday lunch, I thought he had severe indigestion but it turned out to have been a heart attack! Then there was the guitarist boyfriend who ran for an hour every day and would only eat steamed chicken breast with green vegetables in order to look like a stick on stage. He told me this was healthy living—even though he occasionally snorted cocaine and got completely paralytic after four drinks—I suppose that didn't count. He got me jogging, and after a few months I lost about fourteen pounds. But I am completely the wrong build for a runner and eventually slipped a disk trying to keep up. The moral of this is: just start your plan and don't try to include your partner. LIFE'S TOO SHORT TO STOP YOUR PARTNER CREATING THEIR VERY OWN HEART ATTACK— YOU ARE YOUR MAIN PRIORITY! When the weight begins to drop off your stomach, I guarantee that they will start to show an interest and probably join in. Men can't stand being ordered to diet. Most heterosexual men think that bread was designed to have butter on it. If you work out, and do exercises at home, they are going to studiously ignore you, because (for nine men out of ten) it constitutes threatening behavior. Just ignore them and get on with it.

WEEKEND WALKING

The best time to build up your exercise is at the weekends. I try to walk for an hour to two hours every Saturday and Sunday. Join a walking or hiking group and find out about organized walks in your area. Learn how to read a map and buy a guide to walking and hiking trails in your area. Do not be afraid of walking alone, it's a great way of clearing your head and dealing with problems. Walking is the very best exercise there is, and I'm not just writing this because I was president of the Ramblers Association in Britain! People who walk have clear skin, bright eyes, and bags of energy. It doesn't have to be a death march. Start with thirty minutes at a regular pace. Build up very gradually. Buy the right gear to keep warm and dry and you'll find you will enjoy walking all year round.

HOW TO SPEND AN HOUR A DAY EXERCISING WITHOUT REALIZING IT

Buy some small weights of up to six pounds each. Buy an inexpensive exercise bike, secondhand on eBay, or through an ad in the local paper. Or ask at the local gym if they are getting rid of any—often bike machines are chucked out when they introduce new equipment. Position the bike in front of the telly or near a radio. Get up half an hour earlier, get your cup of hot water, and cycle while you listen to the radio or watch the morning news. Thirty minutes will be gone so quickly you won't believe it. You can do arm curls with the weights at the same time. At lunchtime, leave the office and walk briskly for fifteen minutes. When you leave work, walk briskly to the next subway or bus stop, extending this distance every week until you're walking an hour a day. Late at night, you can do some simple exercises for your arms with the weights while you watch some TV. You can also do crunches and core body work while watching TV. I do it while listening to a favorite radio show! There is no point in pretending you have an hour a day to dedicate to exercise. You have to split it up like this. I hate going to a gym or joining any classes; it's just another appointment that I may not be able to keep. Life's too short to fill up your calendar with stuff you then feel bad about canceling. Create your own regime that suits you. Remember that every celebrity who says they spend two hours a day working out is lying through their teeth. Don't they have work to do?

FLEXIBILITY

Flexibility exercises can be done at your desk or while watching TV. Choose an armless, upright chair. When you sit on it, your knees should be on the edge and your feet touching the floor. There are various types of stretching, but for ease and safety, static stretches are recommended here. Stretch major muscle groups to a position of mild discomfort for 10–30 seconds. Perform these stretches two to three days per week, trying to do four repetitions per muscle group.

Seated stretches

Neck
Turn head toward left arm (as though you're smelling your armpit). Grab the back of your head with your left hand and gently pull it toward your armpit until you feel a mild stretch. Hold for 10–30 seconds, then repeat on the opposite side.

Upper back stretch
Hold your arms in front of your body at shoulder height. Rounding your upper back, reach forward with your arms as far as possible and hold for 10–30 seconds.

Arm cross
Sit sideways on your chair and place your hands behind you on your lower back. Try to hold your left elbow with your right hand and your right elbow with your left hand. If this is too difficult, just leave your hands on your lower back and try to push your elbows together.

Shoulder back release
Raise your shoulders toward your ears, hold for 10–30 seconds, then release. Squeeze your shoulder blades together at the back, pinching them together for the same period, and release.

Hamstrings
Sit on the edge of the chair. Straighten one leg and bend the opposite. Keeping a straight back and bending from the hip, lean forward until you feel a mild stretch in the straight leg. Hold for 10–30 seconds and repeat with the opposite leg.

Outer thigh
Sit on the edge of the chair and cross your right leg over the left. Rotate your torso toward the right, hold for 10–30 seconds, and repeat on the opposite side.

Stretches to do in front of the TV

Upper back stretch
Stand up, link your hands together in front of you, and try to separate your shoulder blades by pushing your hands together and your arms away from your body.

Chest stretch
Hold your arm at a 90-degree angle to the wall so that your forearm and hand are against the wall. Turn your chest away from the wall to give a mild stretch across the chest. Repeat on the other side.

Torso
Raise your right arm above your head and bend your torso to the left until you feel a mild stretch on the right side of the body. Hold for a count of five and repeat on the opposite side.

Hamstrings
Lean against a wall, placing your feet two to three feet away from the wall. Bending from the hips and keeping your legs straight, lean forward until you feel a mild stretch at the back of the upper thighs.

Quads
Place your right hand on the wall, bend your right knee, and grasp your left foot with your left hand. Tilt your hips forward until you feel a mild stretch at the front of the thigh—you should feel no pain in the knee. Hold for a count of five and repeat with the other leg.

Calves
Put both hands on the wall. Place your right foot about three feet behind your left foot and push into the wall, keeping the back leg straight, so that you feel a mild stretch at the back of the lower leg. Hold for a count of five and repeat on the other side.

TONING AND STRENGTHENING

Remember muscles don't have brains. They don't care if they are being overloaded with inexpensive weights or fancy equipment, as long as they are placed under some sort of demand. For weight-loss results in the shortest time frame, the exercises need to incorporate more than one muscle group, prompting a cardiovascular response as well as muscular fatigue.

Strength exercises you can do without equipment

Lunges

Start with your legs hip-width apart. Keeping your torso upright, step far enough forward that your front leg is bent at a 90-degree angle to the floor and simultaneously bend your back knee at 90 degrees, without putting it on the floor. Keep your knees over your toes. Hold for a count of two, then push back from the front leg and return to the starting position. Repeat 10–12 times, then rest for 30 seconds and repeat, leading with the other leg.

Squats

For this you can place a chair behind you to sit on, or perform it standing up. Start with your legs hip-width apart. Keeping your torso upright, bend both legs to 90 degrees as if to sit down—do not go farther than 90 degrees and take care to keep your knees over your toes. Hold for a count of two, then straighten your legs back to the starting position. Repeat 10–12 times.

Box push-ups

Start in a box position with your hands and knees on the floor. Keeping your torso rigid, bend your arms at 90 degrees to the floor, and place your chest between your hands. Straighten your arms back to the starting position and repeat 10–12 times. To increase the intensity, lengthen your legs to a full push-up position.

Bridge

Lie on your back on the floor and bend your legs, keeping your feet on the floor. Lift your bottom away from the floor, pulling your bellybutton toward your spine and tucking your bottom under. Hold for a count of five and return to the floor. Repeat 10–12 times.

Back extension

Lie face down on the floor. Keeping your feet on the floor and your eyes looking downward, squeeze your bottom and raise your torso. Squeeze your shoulder blades together and hold for a count of five before lowering to the starting position. Repeat 10–12 times.

You can buy all sorts of gadgets and gimmicks to help you, but it's best to keep it simple and be sceptical of machines that promise results in short spaces of time—they make great coat hangers and gather dust really well.

Things that I've found useful to buy:

- Floor mat
- Moderate weights, 2 to 10 pounds
- Exercise tubing
- Swiss ball (exercise ball)
- Jumprope (if you can jump rope)
- Proper footwear

Household objects that have proved useful:

- Dining room chairs
- Household stairs
- Heavy shopping bags
- Heavy books

- How to shop for food
- Make cooking easy
- Plan meals

LIFE'S TOO
F***ING
SHORT
TO
COOK
LIKE A
TV
CHEF

Here's the deal: I love cooking and I love eating, but I'm not going to let food preparation take over my life. I put together food that tastes great, but doesn't look like a f***ing work of art on the plate. It is good, healthy grub. I've fed pop stars, actors, artists, mad musicians and picky comedians, husbands, lovers, and family, and they all agree my dinners and Sunday lunches are fantastic. So I must be doing something right! Here's how to cook if you're pushed for time, work hard, and have no patience.

First of all, let's take a moment to ask ourselves—what on earth has happened to our relationship with food? When did it stop being something we could all enjoy in an effortless way and start being a way of punishing ourselves? When did we stop eating together? When did we downgrade food into something slightly less interesting than lead-free gasoline? Most women now have a very troubled relationship with what they eat. The majority of us claim to be on a diet, routinely banning wheat, dairy, and all sorts of food from our plates—depending on the last magazine article we read, or the last person we spoke to—but why?

Eating is one of the last great, simple pleasures left in life.

If you go to Italy for your vacation, watch how Italians eat lunch. You don't get a load of miserable women sitting around saying "no" to pasta. Italians delight in using seasonal produce, cooked as simply as possible. Women will eat smaller portions, and they certainly don't smear their bread with butter, but they adore vegetables and fish, prepared with confidence that the basic ingredients are so good they need little dressing up.

The British are mentally sick as a nation when it comes to cooking and presenting food. Never has a nation so lacked confidence in its own cuisine. We've got great vegetables, organic meat, plentiful fish—all available at a farmers' market near you. Available on the bloody Internet if you can't be bothered to go shopping. But the first thing you have to do if you want to eat like I do—enjoying, not loathing food—is **WEAN YOURSELF OFF THE EVIL DRUG OF SUPERMARKETS.** Do you really want to eat food that has been transported halfway around the country to be overpackaged in polystyrene trays and plastic wrap (when Mother Nature has already provided perfectly serviceable naturally biodegradable packaging called skin or rind), and then delivered back to you in fleets of gas-guzzling trucks that clog up our highways? Do you hate food so much that you will only eat vegetables that have been genetically modified so they resemble perfect little doll's food, serried ranks of weenie sweetcorn, baby asparagus the width of a matchstick, and zucchini that wouldn't even fill a mouse?

HOW I HATE MINIATURE VEGETABLES—FOOD FOR PEOPLE WHO HATE FOOD.

We have a crisis about any food that looks a bit knobby, a bit characterful, to the point that supermarkets now often offer it cheaper. God forbid that we might choose to buy vegetables in a market where they sit covered in earth, unwashed, and additive free, naked in all their splendor. One of my favorite places to buy food is the Old Goods Shed in Canterbury, Kent, where stall holders list the names of the farms where the lettuces, potatoes, carrots, and turnips come from and state whether or not they have been sprayed with pesticides. Wherever you live, you can find the nearest farmers' market easily online.

There's nothing shameful or snooty about caring where your food comes from. You are going to put this stuff in your body, the body you spend hundreds of dollars choosing clothes for and slapping cream on in the hope of staving off old age—so why do you care less about who produced the lettuce and eggs you eat than who made your shoes or your shampoo? Why do people covet Jimmy Choo shoes or a Prada bag, delighting in the exquisite workmanship, the beautiful stitching, the fine attention to detail—but then are prepared to eat an oven-ready pizza that is full of additives, a cacophony of fake tastes, chemicals, and processed ingredients? If you care about yourself, then you have to care about food. Simple as that. Change your attitude by going back to basics.

Food, along with sex and relationships, is one of the three most important things in your life.

Life is too short to eat badly, to stuff yourself with s**t, and to cook with no love or care. You owe it to yourself to eat as well as you possibly can.

Don't give me that tired old mantra about "no time." I just don't buy that. If you have no time in your life to buy decent food, to recognize that spending time preparing it and making a delicious meal is absolutely the best way of relaxing, then you are truly sad. I care about where my veggies and meat come from. I don't have a pet, I don't have kids. So you could say I have liberated time for myself to organize the sourcing of decent food. But that shouldn't be impossible for you, too.

JUST PLAN YOUR LIFE SO YOU GET STUFF DELIVERED FROM FARMERS, SUPPLIERS, OR BOX SCHEMES YOU CAN SOURCE ON THE INTERNET, OR VISIT A MARKET ONCE A WEEK. USE SUPERMARKETS ONLY FOR CLEANING PRODUCTS. GET YOUR WINE DELIVERED. INVEST IN FILTERS AND STOP BUYING BOTTLED WATER—IT IS AN OBSCENE WASTE OF MONEY AND THE PLASTIC CONTAINERS POLLUTE THE ENVIRONMENT.

IF YOU ARE GOING TO HAVE PEOPLE ROUND FOR A MEAL, CHOOSE A DATE A WEEK AHEAD SO YOU CAN THINK ABOUT WHAT TO SERVE THEM. IT MUST NEVER BE COMPLICATED, PROMISE ME THAT! FRIENDS ARE COMING ROUND TO ENJOY YOUR COMPANY AND YOUR CONVERSATION, NOT THE BACK OF YOUR HEAD AS YOU BEND OVER THE BLOODY OVEN FOR HOURS ON END.

EATING IN, EATING OUT

A lot of our reluctance to cook at home can be directly traced back to the so-called "revolution" in eating out over the past decade. Now we Brits eat out more than we eat in. But we generally eat rubbish when we eat out. It's either fast food, lacking in nutrition, full of processed ingredients, fake flavorings, or salt and sugar. We put up with this threadbare level of quality in the name of "saving time." Or, when we visit expensive restaurants, quite honestly, generally the stuff we get offered is pathetic. It doesn't matter what food critics say—after all, they've got to keep themselves in work, haven't they? Nine out of ten pubs and restaurants in Britain serve substandard food—precooked, frozen, factory-made. And because we so lack confidence in our own culinary abilities, we don't complain.

BECAUSE WE NO LONGER LEARN HOW TO PREPARE FOOD AT SCHOOL, BECAUSE WE BUY COOKERY BOOKS AS SOME KIND OF VISUAL PORN, AND STILL CAN'T COOK, WE PUT UP WITH POOR FOOD DAY IN AND DAY OUT.

We watch countless television programs about food and have created a group of much-loved celebrity chefs whose antics we thoroughly enjoy and tune in to watch in our millions, but our level of cooking in our own homes has actually declined over the past twenty years. It's all about a lack of confidence, and the restaurant industry capitalizes on our basic insecurities.

In a small Italian seaside resort you go into a café and ask "what's good today?" and they will tell you about the pasta they have made that morning, the fish they had delivered, the game that got shot by local hunters, the ripe tomatoes or the perfect buffalo mozzarella cheese they picked up from a farmer nearby. What's the equivalent in Britain? The laminated menu listing cod in batter with fries and salad, or chicken Kiev? CRIMES AGAINST FOOD.
FOR A COUPLE OF YEARS NOT TOO LONG AGO I WAS THE VOGUE RESTAURANT CRITIC AND I NEVER HAD TO MUNCH MY WAY THROUGH SUCH A LOAD OF PRETENTIOUS CRAP IN MY LIFE!

Why do fashion-conscious chefs insist on piling food up on our plates in ludicrous pyramids with chives fanning out of these perilous constructions like edible propellers? Why do they love to serve us food in horrible giant white bowls the size of chamber pots, as if we are inmates in a Dickensian orphanage? How many times have you been in a restaurant, eagerly awaiting your dinner and been given a melange of ingredients that looks like an edible version of the Sydney Opera House? **THIS IS CUISINE OF THE SICKEST KIND**, and yet critics, TV chefs, and most of us humble customers just sit there and pretend that the lukewarm mishmash in front of us is a groundbreaking culinary masterpiece, when the reality is, it's **CRAP.**

Another of my pet hates about eating out is the horribly pretentious language adopted by restaurateurs who want us to believe that what they are offering is really worth the inflated prices they are charging. In the United Kingdom most of us have our birth certificates written in English, we get married in English, and our funeral ceremonies are conducted in English. But when we go into a restaurant we are confronted with a weird language that bears no relationship to our real world. A kind of Franglais—

as if France was still the place to get the best food in Europe, when it clearly isn't. And in pretentious British restaurants there's a need to tell us the source of every ingredient, generally to justify overpricing. So, scallops are "line-caught" or "ocean-grown." Tomatoes are "sun-ripened" and figs "handpicked." It would be easier to write at the bottom one line that says "all our ingredients are of the highest quality, and organic whenever possible, sourced in the UK if available," but of course that is just too bald a statement. Then there's every chance the menu will contain items that there's not a snowball's chance in hell of you knowing what they are, creating the ideal opportunity for the waiter to be as patronizing as possible, shrinking you down to the lowly level where he clearly thinks you belong. I'm talking about things like "pithiviers" or "financiers"—cookies, waffles, crêpes, who gives a f*** what they are? They could be top hats for all we know. Life's too short to put yourself through this ritual humiliation.

PROMISE ME YOU WILL NEVER RETURN TO ANY RESTAURANT THAT INFLICTS PYRAMIDS, MENU TWADDLE, OR MYSTERY INGREDIENTS ON YOU, AND MAKE SURE YOU TELL THE OWNER WHY YOU ARE LEAVING.

Three of the few professionals in Britain who write as if they love cooking real food, and actually eating it, are Simon Hopkinson, Nigel Slater, and Hugh Fearnley-Whittingstall. You'll never see them dish up anything in a f***ing pyramid. They constantly talk about using ingredients that are in season, not tropical fruit and out-of-season peas that have been air-freighted halfway around the world. Eat at Jeremy Lee's Blueprint Café in London and there won't be a pile on your plate, just top ingredients beautifully cooked. Because of the claptrap we put up with when eating out, we make the fateful mistake of thinking that's how we have to cook at home for other people. FORGET IT!

THE JOY OF COOKING

So when you cook, please forget everything you have to go through when eating out. When you are cooking at home, you are in charge, you are creating the agenda. Read a book like Nigel Slater's *The Kitchen Diaries* and you will begin to understand how to cook what is in season, how to use leftovers, how to put together meals that are simple that rely on a short list of good-quality ingredients.

ONCE YOU HAVE GOOD GREENS, THEN ANY MEAL IS ABOUT A HUNDRED PERCENT SIMPLER.

I have gone back to growing some vegetables, but only in small, manageable raised beds about two yards square. I will never go back to keeping a huge vegetable garden like I did decades ago. It ruined my back, and all I did was produce gluts, resulting in hours spent making jams and chutneys. I grow a few lettuces, beans, red chard, spinach, radishes, mizuna, and arugula, basically because they're really easy and I refuse to eat anything that's been picked miles away, washed in chemicals, and stuck in a plastic bag. You can even grow this stuff in window boxes or upended halves of old pipes.

FILL YOUR FRIDGE WITH GOOD INGREDIENTS.

My rule of thumb is to fill the fridge with the best vegetables, fresh herbs, and fruit I can afford (that's the starting point for eating well at home), plus cans of peas and beans—life's certainly too short to start soaking them (the exception is lentils, which you can cook from scratch in half an hour). But I keep a small supply of condiments, plus hot chili paste, tomato purée, pasta, rice, couscous, and bulgur wheat. The only other stuff I buy every week is good yogurt and free-range eggs. That's it. I only buy meat and fish when I am going to eat it—that way you eat less meat and it's always fresh.

WHAT I COOK

My favorite food when friends are coming round is a really good free-range chicken, cut down the backbone and spread out, then roasted in a big roasting pan with loads of whole heads of garlic, potatoes cut up in their skins, olive oil, and thyme. Or I put the chicken in a large pasta pot with a bunch of herbs, celery, onions, and a couple of carrots, cover it with water, bring it slowly to the boil, let it bubble hard for a couple of minutes, then turn off the heat, put a heavy lid on it, cover it with a couple of dishtowels to keep the heat in, and leave it for an hour. It will be perfectly poached, and can taste delicious warm or cold. All you have to do then is whiz up some mayo in the blender with good olive oil and fresh eggs—really hard to f*** up if you dribble the oil in slowly. Serve with potatoes you brought to the boil in their skins on top of the stove and then drained and stuck in the oven in a covered pan for an hour at 300°F. Are you beginning to get the idea? My rule is: very little effort, not a stack of pots and pans all boiling away furiously on the top of the stove. If you don't like potatoes, you can cook rice the same way, from boiling point, and let it finish really slowly in the oven, then stir in toasted nuts or raisins.

Sometimes I make a starter on a large dish (I got a huge tin tray in IKEA for less than $10 that makes a great platter) using different kinds of salad leaves, arranged by type, another dish of anchovies, and some hard-boiled eggs with chopped cilantro. Stick a bottle of olive oil, a jar of mustard, and some white balsamic vinegar on the table and let everyone make their own salad.

I do hardly any stove-top cooking at all—I don't want to get a red face and sore arms from hours of stirring. I tend to start things on a high heat and then leave them in a medium–low oven (300°F) until I need them. I'll have a bath, set the table, play some music, drink a glass of wine. Always remind yourself: eating is enjoyable, not an opportunity to feel inadequate.

Buy a shoulder of lamb at the weekend, turn it briefly in hot oil, just to brown it, then take about 4 cups of finely chopped onions, carrots, celery, and leeks (whiz them all in the blender to save time) and brown them in the pan you used for the lamb, adding more oil if you have to. Chuck in thyme or rosemary, and garlic. Then, take the veggies and put them in a big roasting pan, bung the meat on top, season with salt and pepper, pour over half a bottle of white wine, and cover with two layers of foil. Leave it in the oven at 300°F for at least 4 hours. At some stage you can toss in some potatoes in another roasting pan, to cook in their skins. Or a pot of brown rice you brought to a boil first, tightly sealed. Go out, have fun, have Sunday afternoon sex, read a book, watch a crap DVD. Your food will be ready when you are. Just stir-fry some spinach for 30 seconds or fast-boil some green beans at the last minute, and that's it. The meat will fall off the bone, and the sauce will be fantastic—you can mash up a bit of it in the blender and stir it back in to thicken it. Why should cooking be any more trouble than that?

Plums and rhubarb are fruits that can be cooked very slowly in the oven and then served with thick yogurt, but my favorite dessert is baked figs. Place them in a small flameproof dish you rubbed with a bit of butter. Just cut a cross on top of each fig, sprinkle with brown sugar, and add a glug of Marsala if you have some, water if not. Cook for 20 minutes in a hot oven, or around 40 minutes if you're putting it in the oven that's cooking the lamb.

I am not one of those people who can only eat fish if it's got the head chopped off. I love making fish stew, but it's a weekend dish as it does take time to do properly. I make a fish stock from bones and bits with celery, onions, and herbs, bubbling it for an hour, then cooling it and straining it. I generally do it the day before, but it doesn't matter. For the stew I fry some finely chopped onions with saffron and garlic, taking care not to let them brown. I add a couple of cans of chopped tomatoes, the fish stock, some hot paprika or a dab of chili paste, and let it bubble away for 45 minutes. Then I add sliced red potatoes and the starch in them thickens my soup. Finally, when the potatoes are almost cooked, I add my fish—the thickest pieces first (it's up to you, just reckon on four big chunks per person). They

I hope this encourages you to take the plunge and

cook in 5 minutes. The stew must only be bubbling slightly as you finally add any shellfish—shrimp, clams, mussels—otherwise they will disintegrate. Take the pot off the stove, cover it for 5 minutes, and it's all ready. I serve it with toasted bread, some grated Emmenthaler cheese, if I can find it, and a dish of blender-made mayo to which I've added loads of crushed garlic and paprika to make it really hot. When I cooked this on television I beat Gordon Ramsay in a blind tasting—he wasn't very pleased! It looks good and isn't hard to make.

If I want to eat fish and haven't got the time to make a stew, then I just ask the fishmonger what's freshest (I never eat farmed salmon or bass, I'd rather eat something that's had a more interesting life) and then I just stick it in an oiled dish, head on, dribble oil over, cover with foil, and bake for up to 30 minutes in a hot oven, depending on how thick the fish is. When you stick a knife in and the flesh comes away from the bone, it's done.

I eat all types of game—it's free range, low fat, tastes delicious, and never takes more than 45 minutes to cook. Gorgeous white-fleshed partridges, baked in a covered casserole with shredded cabbage and juniper berries. Pheasants, casseroled with celery and thyme. Grouse, roasted for 10 minutes, with brown rice to soak up all the lovely juices. Guinea fowl, split down the backbone, baked on a bed of grapes, dribbled with olive oil. Wild duck, split and painted with marmalade, then roasted in a very hot oven for 15 minutes. What's not to love about any of that?

For convenience, I cook up a load of lentils and then keep them in a container in the fridge to eat with different things during the week when I'm working. When I'm filming, I take a plastic container of my own lunch whenever I can—I only eat a sandwich or sushi when I've gotten up too late, too hungover to do this! If you stir-fry spinach, chard, or turnip tops for 30 seconds with some chile pepper and add them to canned lentils, you've got something delicious. For a great salad, mix chopped red onions and parsley into a can of rinsed canned beans, then dress with top-quality olive oil.

treat cooking as a pleasure rather than a chore.

SATURDAY LUNCH SHOULD BE EFFORTLESS. I HAVE SEVERAL PASTA DISHES WHICH EXPAND TO FILL WHOEVER IS AROUND AND DON'T INTERRUPT THE READING OF THE NEWSPAPERS.

For a quick crab pasta buy fresh crabmeat—one crab shell full feeds about three people—cilantro, a bunch of scallions, a long hot red chile pepper, and a couple of fat cloves of garlic, peeled and chopped. Use wholewheat spaghetti—one packet feeds about six people. Chop up the scallions—I always do this with kitchen scissors, and use them to roughly snip up the cilantro, too, to avoid extra dishwashing. Also cut up the chile, chucking out the seeds if you don't want it too hot. Soften the onion, garlic, and chile in a heavy skillet, add the crabmeat, mashing it in, and using all the brown meat as well as the white. Add the cilantro and a glass of white wine (any old leftovers will do), plus a generous pinch of cayenne pepper. Leave to stew on low heat for 5 minutes. Cook the pasta and at the last minute stir a big tablespoon of cream or crème fraîche into the crab. Drain the pasta and mix it all together in the hot pot you cooked the pasta in, then adjust the seasoning and serve. A meal in 10 minutes. Serve it with a salad made with Belgian endive, frisée, Bibb lettuce, red-leaf lettuce—the more bitter the leaves the better—topped with some crushed walnuts and loads of olive oil and lemon juice.

For another quick pasta dish, get some small fresh tomatoes—do not keep them in the fridge—and put them in a roasting pan, covering the bottom of it. Strew with sprigs of thyme you have crushed between your fingers to bruise, loads of olive oil, a dollop of balsamic vinegar, a couple of pinches of sugar, black pepper, salt. Roast at 400°F for 20 to 30 minutes, until the tomatoes' skins pop and they start to caramelize. Cook the pasta. Put the tomatoes in a heavy skillet and, if they are too liquid, place over high heat to quickly reduce them to a syrup. Mix the tomatoes with the pasta, adding loads of black pepper, and serve—delicious!

Just have fun. Forget Nigella Lawson's cake recipes—we haven't got the face she has to go on top of the massive hips that result from eating teatime treats. We haven't got her willpower to eat only one. Forget hours of preparation. Forget trying to make intricate sauces and complicated pastries.

Create your own small repertoire.
Eat well.
But above all, make it simple.

LIFE'S TOO F***ING SHORT TO BELIEVE WHAT MEN SAY

- How to understand your partner
- When to fake it
- How to compromise

I adore and value the company of men—God knows I have lived with a whole range of them nearly all my adult life from the age of eighteen, been married four times, and had three relationships that have lasted over four years each. I'd call myself a serial monogamist. Or you could say I'm eternally optimistic. Or bonkers. Or you could ask what kind of weird person would want to live with a self-centered workaholic like me, who has a close circle of friends who are pretty similar, who spends a large part of her time in the company of gay men, and who is definitely not interested in family life of any description?

One thing's for sure—there is no chance of me discovering latent lesbian tendencies in later life. I'm one hundred percent heterosexual, although I know that I'm an easy character to spoof at drag balls! In spite of what's been written about me, I am not at war with men. I do not see the point in routinely trashing the male sex. Men have helped me as close friends, as lovers, and in the workplace. But I do think it takes a lot of thinking to get the best out of them. If only it was just as simple as lining up a great shag!

I have spent all my working life surrounded by men, as I have hacked my way through the media jungle. In my chosen fields, men have been the majority of my managers, although that is changing. When I started out as a journalist in the sixties, I had to learn how to work alongside the opposite sex. I wasn't much better at managing this than I was at sorting out my love life, but I have made progress over the years! This chapter is an attempt to try and pass on what I've found out about coexisting with men as lovers, friends, and fellow workers: I invite you to share some of my successes and my disasters—make of them what you will!

CHEMISTRY

Only the other day I was trying on a pair of XL sweat pants in the men's department of a trendy T-shirt shop in Paris, when a middle-aged man sitting on a sofa outside the changing room (waiting for his son) told me that size M had looked better as I had a great body. I was incredulous—but there you go. The trick is to accept a compliment gracefully, with a small smile, not anything that will encourage further ridiculous flattery, and not react negatively and treat the man involved as a revolting pervert. Sadly, I fell into the latter category, and complained to the gorgeous twenty-three-year-old sales assistant at the cash register about being "harassed." Later, the

The first thing to remember is that no matter how self-critical you may be, how loathsome you may find your body, someone out there will always fancy you!

man I was having lunch with pointed out that I had chosen to change in the male area of the shop, and if I found a friendly comment offensive, why didn't I wear a burqa?

A friend once said I was a gay man trapped in a woman's body.

There is an element of truth in that—I certainly don't think or generally act in a particularly feminine way, or what was traditionally regarded as female. Perhaps this "male" way of thinking started when my father decided to treat me as the son he'd never had, and take me to football matches and speedway racing every week until I was about eleven. I hated dolls, and when I was given one I ripped the arms out of her sockets in a fit of pique. The dismembered object was immediately despatched to the Dolls' Hospital in Fulham Broadway. The following Christmas I was thrilled to unwrap a big box containing a complicated Meccano set, and Dad and I set about building a giant crane. Soon afterward he announced that I had the makings of an engineer—and throughout my time at high school Dad had high hopes that I would be following in his footsteps. He was delighted when I decided to study architecture, and appalled when I dropped out after two years to become a journalist.

At architectural college there were just five or six girls in my year, and nearly a hundred boys. In this male environment I capitalized on my looks by wearing very short skirts at every opportunity. I was a weird mixture of brash self-confidence and extreme insecurity—still true today. I realized straightaway that **the majority of heterosexual men never communicate their feelings in any straightforward way,** and that many of my fellow students had left home for the first time and couldn't even boil an egg or make themselves some toast, but they could provide me with correct answers for my college exams in plumbing and structural mechanics.

Most of the men I've spent my life with certainly never revealed any emotions, unless it was about sport or cars or motorcycles or fishing equipment. I could never understand the nature of any of my sexual relationships—and I certainly forced myself on a lot of men, inviting myself to live with them, deciding I would like to get married or engaged, and easing them into my plans for our relationship, rather than the other way around. I admit that

I, too, am reluctant about revealing the true nature of my feelings—because the more you give away, the weaker your position in any ensuing arguments or disagreements. LIFE'S TOO SHORT TO DISSECT THE NITTY-GRITTY OF YOUR LOVE LIFE. Too much knowledge is unnerving and draining. Just accept the raw material you've got—you won't be able to change your partner very much, and not at all if they're over thirty.

MEN AT WORK

It's the same at work—it's almost impossible to change the mentality of the men you work with. Better to work around them, recognize their weaknesses, but don't draw attention to their shortcomings. Accept that you are going to have to work fifty percent harder to get where you want if men are your managers. More women may be getting into middle management, but the pay gap is actually getting wider, not smaller, in some professions. Don't get as irritated, as I regularly do, when the men at work think that some blonde airhead who's just arrived in the office is the greatest thing since sliced bread.

Once you're over forty, you can be witty, intelligent, powerful, and hard working, but you will not be the person the middle-aged bloke at the top is interested in.

You will not be the person he wants to have lunch with or pop down to the pub with after work to share office gossip. There are some female writers at the newspapers I've worked for who routinely churn out mind-numbing f***ing drivel about their latest hairstyle, the length of their bangs, who they shagged last night, or their eco-friendly toilet paper. And they get top billing. They just happen to be attractive, smiley, and under thirty-five. I could be bitter, but what's the point? I earn more anyway. The editor thinks they're gorgeous and slaps their picture all over the front page in the pathetic belief that they'll sell more newspapers. No point in giving it a second thought.

At work, men never tell you the truth about what they are really thinking and what their strategies are.

They love congregating in groups, jangling keys in their pockets, discussing the minutiae of a sporting event or the intricacies of a particular car journey. Luckily, normal women are not blessed with the need to indulge in any of this, which frees us up for at least thirty minutes a day for stuff we'd rather be doing like shopping online, or reading magazines. I know this may sound sexist, but everywhere I have worked, men just do this stuff—chattering away to each other like chickens in a coop. It is a mistake to attempt to show any interest or join in—pretending you're one of the chaps will get you nowhere socially (other women at work will loathe you), and certainly won't improve your career.

MEMORY GAPS

Most men have very selective memories. Whether it is at home or in the office, when asked to do something, they often claim that you "didn't tell them." Rubbish. **THE MALE BRAIN IS HARD-WIRED SO THEIR MENTAL CIRCUITRY WILL NEVER ACCEPT SOME REQUESTS.**

It might be changing a toilet roll—something the male physique finds almost impossible to do. It might be loading the dishwasher correctly and subsequently switching it on. It might be separating out the washing into the right categories, putting it in the machine, and starting the appropriate program. Men who run big businesses and lead teams of dozens of people, who handle complex issues at work and manage millions of dollars, generally find any of the above as incomprehensible as you or I would find building a space shuttle to Mars. Men will never bother to learn how to operate the timer on your oven, or learn how the central-heating control box works. When it comes to this stuff, those arms (that are so good at issuing orders, or making love to you from time to time) are about as useful as the flippers on a baby seal.

DON'T EVEN ATTEMPT TO ARGUE, JUST ACCEPT THE REALITY THAT WOMEN DO THIS STUFF BETTER. GET EVEN IN OTHER WAYS.

I read once that men and women should set aside time, a special moment when, over a glass of wine or a cup of tea, you chat about the upcoming week, what your individual commitments are and enter them on a calendar you keep in the kitchen. HA F***ING HA. THIS NEVER WORKS. For two years now I have endeavored to do this—and every now and then, I tell my partner about vacations, important things we ought to go to together. I carefully write entries on a calendar we keep in a prominent place in the kitchen (just like all my girlfriends do), writing carefully in pencil so that it can be erased and altered—concerts I got tickets for, train schedules, hotel bookings, arrival times at airports. And what happens? If I mention over breakfast on a Sunday what I think might be happening over the next few days, I can absolutely guarantee that within two minutes I'll have a pink-faced baby bawling at me across the table, "I never bloody well agreed to that—you never told me we were doing so and so…"

It's all down to women's superior ability to multitask and retain instructions and information in our memories at different levels. To get men to do certain things, you may have to remind them ten times—especially if it is one of the tasks I've listed above that they secretly loathe. You can start by writing a list on a Post-it note, then sticking it on the back of the front door every single day. They will walk around it. Tunnel vision. Selective input. Whatever you want to call it.

HOME TRUTHS

And let's not even get wound up about the touchy subject of buying food! Men take your shopping list out of the front door, nonchalantly stuffing it in the back pocket of their jeans, and then lose it between home and the supermarket, returning triumphantly several hours later with ten bags crammed full of stuff THEY not YOU thought was needed. You find the list, like a discarded piece of origami, lying on the front seat of the car, unread. It's enough to make you weep—but what's the answer?

Life's too short to constantly complain about all the myriad ways men fail at these tasks we want them to do. Don't even try to reshape, train, or alter their conduct. Leave it to professionals.

It has been scientifically proven that when women enter supermarkets they shop more quickly and more accurately, they have better spatial memories of where required items are in the store. Don't take over all these tasks yourself in the name of efficiency—are you mad? If you make loads of extra work for yourself, you'll be shattered. Order as much as you can via the Internet. Only take your own clothes to the dry cleaners. Only iron what you need for yourself and the kids. Find (or suggest) a laundry—he can pay for his stuff to be ironed. Or barter—if he does some stuff then you'll do something in return.

Take cooking—some men are good at whisking up a few comfort foods, like making bread, cooking spaghetti bolognese, or putting together steak, salad, and fries. Okay, he's not Jamie Oliver or Gordon Ramsay, but surely it's better than doing it yourself?

DON'T SNEER, BUILD ON THIS SMALL BEGINNING.

Let him choose what you are eating one day a week, and then he can buy it and cook it. It's not your problem, and it will hardly f*** up your healthy eating regime once in seven days.

There have been too many times in my life—and I suspect yours—when I've just got on with cooking the supper because no one else was going to do it. Those days are over. Now I eat what I want, buy what I want, cook when I want. It's fit in or f*** off time.

When men come up with that classic phrase "stop nagging me, I'm going to get around to doing this in my own time," we all know what the three magic words my own time really mean: this year, next year, sometime, generally never. It's one of the few simple and one hundred percent guaranteed ways men exercise power and control over women. My best advice in this situation:

JUST FEEL INWARDLY SUPERIOR—
BECAUSE YOU ARE!

As a result of working in television and the print media for many years and issuing complicated instructions to large teams of people, I have developed the unfortunate knack of saying everything I want done three times. The first time, you issue the order, outlining what you want done. The second time, you repeat it, but this time breaking the task down into simple sections so they can't f*** it up. The third time, you go through it all over again, putting in a slightly edited version to hold the bloke's attention and make sure that you are both singing from the same hymnal. Believe me, it does generally take this amount of repetition to enact one simple task with the minimum amount of f*** ups, to achieve a result conforming as nearly as possible to your requirements. If this works in newspaper offices, television studios, with film crews, and in editing suites, then it will generally work at home. The challenge is trying not to sound like a dictator or world-class nag, both of which I have been accused of in the past (with plenty of justification). From taking out the trash to watering the plants to setting the table to sorting the washing, any domestic task will take a minimum of three repeats of an initial order. Any less and you can start celebrating your good fortune!

WHAT MEN SAY AND WHAT THEY MEAN ARE TWO COMPLETELY DIFFERENT THINGS.

There was a best-selling book called *Men Are From Mars, Women Are From Venus* in which the author argued that men and women use language in very different ways. Women just say what they want, whereas men are far more oblique and circumspect. And because of this, all sorts of misunderstandings and grievances result. The part of the book that really irritated me was the "help" issued to women about how to phrase requests to men so that they will rise to the bait and do what we want. It always seemed to involve a piece of flattery or cajoling. Banned were crisp, clear orders, as in: "Take the f***ing trash out, it's the sixth time I've asked you and the smell is disgusting." Instead we're supposed to say something like: "Honey, I know you are really busy watching that television show, but when you have a moment, do you think you could try and take out the trash?" Instead of issuing a simple everyday command like: "Don't forget on your way home to pick up pizza or Chinese takeout for supper as I am working," we are supposed to turn this request into something resembling a UN peace negotiation by phrasing it thus: "Sweetheart, I know you've got a really tough day ahead, but I would really appreciate it if on the way home you could…etc."

HAVE YOU STOPPED LAUGHING YET AT THE SHEER IMPRACTICALITY OF THIS?

You and I both know that life's too short to enter into a lot of gushing verbiage about something as basic as buying supper. Nine times out of ten I guarantee he'll forget no matter what approach you take.

There are many simple solutions that protect your sanity:

* You could get your own dinner.
    * You could cook a big meal earlier in the week and eat leftovers.
* Order takeout and text him to collect it.
    * Order takeout to be delivered—and only order enough for yourself.

Over the years I have learned, to my cost, that

THE MORE YOU APPEAR WILLING TO DOWN TOOLS, STOP THE WORK ON THINGS YOU WANT TO DO, GO INTO THE KITCHEN AND PUT TOGETHER AN EVENING MEAL, THE MORE EVERYONE IN THE HOUSEHOLD WILL EXPECT IT.

COOKING MUST BE A PLEASURE, NOT A CHORE.

MEN AND TIME

Obviously men do not operate on the same clock as women, just as they do not speak the same language. When men say the word "soon" it can mean all sorts of things. "Soon" home from work is very different from doing the dishes "soon." Basically, "soon" is whatever they want it to mean—a long time if they're enjoying themselves doing something else, or it could be a a minute or two, if they've nothing more interesting on the horizon.

"SOON" is one of the words women are right to treat with utter contempt. Coming from a bloke, it is meaningless.

THE FEMALE CLOCK

Over the years, a subtle form of brainwashing has gone on that reinforces the stereotype that women like gossiping and shopping and are always late. Nonsensical bilge designed to ensure we don't rise above our station. I am only late by other people's agenda, not my own. I don't want to walk into a pub or café or restaurant and sit by myself, so I always arrive a little bit late, maybe five minutes—what's the crime in that? Hardly a flogging offence—my reasoning seems perfectly sensible!

TELLING THE TRUTH IS OVERRATED. Never look for

veracity in every aspect of a relationship—we all lie about everything all the time. Life's too short to conduct a detective-style investigation every day

about what your partner has been up to and why he is late.

Men lie about where they've been and who they've been with—but what's the point of getting annoyed about it? Be honest, do you really want to have to tell the truth about what you spend your

money on, what your new coat or shoes cost? And I am the first to admit that when it comes to putting out my partial version of the truth, I am an expert—how else could I remain friends with so many of my exes? Take sex, what's the f***ing point in offering an honest evaluation of the f*** you've just had? Why not just let out a satisfied sigh, and masturbate later? I've had great sex, boring sex, drunken sex, dreary sex, and inconsequential sex. I'm not a relationship counselor, but I do know that over the years sex with the same person goes off the boil and other things have to replace it. You can only improve sex marginally, not fundamentally, if your partner is disinterested or lackluster. Far more important in the long term is a shared sense of humor, kindness, and considerate behavior.

In short, men are not our enemies, but a great resource—it's harnessing all that, so that our lives are not disrupted to an unacceptable level by trying to accommodate and cater to them, that's the difficult part. Dealing with men successfully can be draining, infuriating, and wearing. But it's worth it!

LONDON DIARY

★

*ADDRESS and
1966 ENGAGEMENTS
BOOK*

katharine

I'm a celeb
Nov - Dec 2004

address book

Silvine

MEMO BOOK

TRAVEL JOURNAL

LIFE'S TOO F***ING SHORT TO TALK TO PEOPLE WHO ARE BORING

schoolmates

- Cull the deadwood
- "Work mates" are just that
- Accept that your friends won't all get on
- And be prepared to hear about YOUR shortcomings

How many friends do you really need? How much of your week do you waste talking to people who bore the crap out of you? Let's divide our lives into two categories—the people you have to communicate with in order to work, shop, and deal with the practicalities of daily living, and then the people who enhance our lives, give us something we crave, make us laugh, offer us ideas, emotional support, or simply a comforting feeling of familiarity.

RULE NUMBER ONE Do not muddle up the people you have to communicate with in category one with real friends. Be careful not to try and please too many people as you go through each and every day—it will be thoroughly draining and you are on a hopeless mission, believe me. When I was appointed editor of a national newspaper, the previous editor was fired that morning and then I was brought in to address the staff and rally morale. I received an excellent piece of advice, which was: in any work situation, one third of the people you encounter will instinctively loathe you on sight—give up on them and don't waste any energy. Just reduce matters to pleasantries, the bare minimum needed to be courteous. The second third will have decided they like you and will broadly go along with what you want. Great! But they are not your friends, they are "work mates," which is a whole heap of difference. The remaining third are where you put your effort in—you will be able to persuade them to work with you and agree with what you want to do—and as a result you will have a two-thirds majority in the workplace and be able to run it your way, put through your plans, and persuade them to sign on to your ideas. This means you only have to put time and effort into wooing one third of everyone you work with.

RULE NUMBER TWO

Be decisive about how you spend your time at work and outside it. Don't waffle. Cut meetings to the minimum, stick to a list, allot people a short time to say their bit, but make a decision at the end of the time, and stick to it. We don't live in a collective—someone's got to run things from the front, and if it's you, stop worrying about whether people like you or not, and bloody well get on with it. Apply the same rule to people you talk to outside work, about getting things fixed, shopping, running the shit that's modern living. You don't need to be friends with the plumber or electrician to get something fixed. You aren't the greengrocer or butcher's best friend—you're a valued customer. Be civil, keep that friendly banter to an acceptable minimum, otherwise they'll know too much about you. Life's too short!

RULE NUMBER THREE Be very clear about what
real friends are, as opposed to "work mates." Friends are the people who don't need to know you. They aren't impressed by you. They are prepared to tell you things that no one else (not even your partner) would have the cheek to tell you. Friends tell you when you look like a dog in a dress, when your roots need doing, when your latest shag is a complete embarrassment. Friends are not sycophants—after all, they've got better things to do with their busy lives than sit around sucking up to you.

DON'T EXPECT ALL YOUR FRIENDS TO LIKE EACH OTHER, WANT TO SPEND TIME TOGETHER, FIT TOGETHER IN ONE BIG HAPPY GROUP.

FRIENDS matter,

RULE NUMBER FOUR Make sure that,

even though you only see real friends very occasionally, they realize
that they mean a lot to you. It might only be sending them a postcard
every few months, but don't let your friendship wither to extinction.
I have friends who I have known since I went to college over forty years
ago. I have friends from every decade of my life, and every relationship. But
I can't see them all, all the time. And I understand that they've got friends
from every aspect of their lives, too, and can't fit me in at short notice
when I am having a low moment. Friends require patience and tolerance—
neither of which I am any good at! At the same time, be realistic about how
much time you've got in any one week for friends—don't say you'll do
something with them out of guilt because you feel pressurized into it.
Make a date further in the future and make it something special that you've
put on your calendar and cleared time for. I have some friends that I might
only see once a year, but because we have known each other so long, we
can pick up the conversation as though we last spoke yesterday. I will go and
stay with them, or we might spend the weekend together, or we might go
out for a meal, or a long walk.

Believe me, I have had four husbands and lived with three men for over
four years each, and the one constant thing in my life has been my friends.
They matter far more to me in the long term than any of my relatives; in
fact, my friends are my true family. You have to adopt a different set of
rules for dealing with those related to you by blood, and in that I freely
admit I have always been completely hopeless. My friends are my peers,
and the only people I feel completely relaxed with. When I am old, it will
be friends that I spend my time with.

RULE NUMBER FIVE

Don't feel guilty about dumping people when you copy one address book into the next. As you go through life you will naturally make new friends and discard others. You've only got time for a handful of close friends on a regular basis. Accept that you will lose touch with some people, because you've stopped having anything in common.

RUTHLESSLY ANALYZE YOUR ADDRESS BOOK, CHUCK OUT PEOPLE YOU HAVEN'T SEEN FOR TWO YEARS. START A NEW BOOK AND ONLY PUT IN THE PEOPLE YOU REALLY WANT TO SEE.

EDIT OUT:

* The worthies
* The bores
* The dreary school friends who married gray people
* Your mum's next-door neighbor when you were a kid
* Your secretaries from decades ago
* That nice man you once slept with out of pity

DO SERIOUS PRUNING. WE CAN'T LIVE OUR LIVES IN THE PAST—I HATE MEMORY LANE.

"WORK MATES" change.

Friends that constantly harp on about some golden era when you were both fourteen and who now think that life has treated them badly are a f***ing drag. Friendship is about coping with the present, and looking forward to the future—that way you will always appear youthful, animated, interested. It's fun to reminisce, but in small doses. I accept that other people will edit me out of their lives, too—it's tough, but you have to accept that our lives change and friendships can wane. Don't persist with that insane idea we all grew up with at school—HAVING A BEST FRIEND. It SUCKS. What happens when that "best friend" gets tired of you, your agenda, your life, your problems? Then you're in deep shit. Best to nurture and sustain a handful of friends, and the group will change gradually over the years.

RULE NUMBER SIX Don't shirk dealing with boring people you don't want to talk to (and realize that sometimes you and I, dear reader, are bloody boring, too). Edit overcommunication out of your life. Don't waste time conjuring up elaborate excuses for not responding to phone messages. Just don't reply—unless it is to say you're sorry, you're busy, and leave it at that.

Texting is just as bad. Why get repetitive strain injury prolonging a series of dopey jokes in txt spk? My solution is just to switch the phone off. Every week I get a text message from an artist (who I really like, but who has only one person on her agenda and that is herself) telling me to read her column in *The Independent*. She writes it every Friday and then presses the "send all" button. It drives me MAD, and so I send her a text back saying, "Did you f***ing bother to read my column in *The Independent* yesterday? That's how I earn my living in case you haven't noticed." If anyone sends me a round-robin e-mail, I simply delete them from my list. Ditto e-mails containing jokes or recommendations about websites or blogs.

Life's too f***ing short to log on and read some other sad cow's story about getting up, washing her hair, and dealing with a grouchy boss in the office. Delete!!

Blogs are a way of avoiding making friends. You've got all these pals in cyberspace—but so what? They aren't going to come round when you've been dumped, open a bottle of wine, and make you laugh. They won't be there for you when you need them.

My true friends have been constant through all my different jobs, my relationships, my houses, my unflattering hairstyles. So what do you do if one of them suddenly embarks on a relationship with a total bore? You have to go with the flow—after all, you will have done the same thing and inflicted a toy boy or a brain-dead moron on them in your time. Try and find ways to meet your mates by themselves—I always say, "let's have a girls night out" or "let's have a heart to heart" if they are male, and we go for a drink or supper with no partners in tow and have a thoroughly fantastic

Jude Deb

me & Anne

three hours moaning about relatives, relationships, work, why we are fat, how the stupidest f***ing cow we ever worked with now runs the television station and so on.

Let's be honest. The best nights out are like this— without any partners.

I have a friend who is a newspaper columnist and we have dinner together every couple of months. It is invaluable to her and me.

RULE NUMBER SEVEN
IF YOU PROMISE A FRIEND A NIGHT WHERE THE TWO OF YOU ARE GOING TO HAVE AN INTIMATE CHAT, STICK TO IT. NEVER, EVER, INVITE SOMEONE ELSE ALONG.

Sooner or later, the unfortunate boyfriend or partner will be painlessly shed by your friend, and you can commiserate. Or, if the partnership lasts a year or longer, you'd better start re-evaluating and see if there's anything about them you can tolerate! Let your girlfriends moan about their husbands and how their sex life is hopeless, but don't fall into the trap of comprehensively trashing men. That's so unattractive, and also, in the long run, not a great strategy. We know men have all sorts of shortcomings and limitations, but if you're not gay, then you have to find a way to work around them and utilize what they CAN do.

Most important of all and RULE NUMBER EIGHT
Try to stay pals with your ex-husbands and boyfriends after you've gone your separate ways. If you loved them so much you shagged them for months or even years, then how come they are now a pile of shit just because you've split up? It's tough on your friends, many of whom will really like your ex, and, in fact, might like your ex a whole heap more than they like you! There is only one ex in my life who I can't bear to see again, and as all my friends thought I'd lost my marbles when I married him in Las Vegas, drunk, in the middle of the night, around the time I was fifty, it's no bad thing. Obviously your exes may end up marrying or living with people you find a bit of a drag, but that doesn't mean you can't be civil to each other. I adore my second husband's wife, and I'm a useless godmother to one of their sons. I get on really well with this ex-husband—because I'm not married to him.

RULE NUMBER NINE
Define the limits of friendship. Do not let friends take over your life and boss you into doing things you don't want to do. If they ask you to an event you can't face, just graciously decline, claiming you're doing something else. If they are going to invite you to supper, don't feel you have to cook for them in return if you're too busy. Arrange to meet in a wine bar or cheap diner where you can pay, when you want.

DON'T FEEL GUILTY.

You need time by yourself, but you need time with friends, too. Make sure you keep a balance.

MAKING NEW FRIENDS

Shared interests is the best route. Evening classes, sports, games like bridge, mahjong, or Scrabble, movies, theater. Sign up for a cookery course, go on vacations where you travel in a group. Become part of a book club, which is what loads of my girlfriends love doing, and if there isn't one where you work or live, why not start one? When I went to my local theater I realized that joining the drama group was a really big source of friends for loads of people. You have to remember—you will never be the stupidest or the least talented person there, and you can always make props or help with costumes.

Forget about meeting people at the local pub, too much gossip and no privacy. I go to flea markets, antique fairs, and rummage sales, and in the process of collecting have met loads of interesting people. I have become friends with people I've met at museum events, talks, and lectures, but the cast-iron way to make friends, in my humble opinion, is through walking. Join a local walking club, and if the groups in your area seem a bit too elderly, go online and check out the groups catering to younger people. For someone who has spent their entire life working in the media, I have made very few close friends through work. I have a huge contact book, plenty of men and women I could call acquaintances—but far fewer true friends.

PLEASE UNDERSTAND—WHEN YOU FINISH WORK EACH DAY YOUR BRAIN NEEDS TO SWITCH OFF.

That's where friends come in—they supply input.

The exception for me was making a television program called *Network 7* in the mid-1980s. It was such a slog, and we worked every hour of the day in a dilapidated warehouse in London's East End. At the end of a year, a gang of us went on vacation together—all we did was sleep, drink, eat, and lie on the sand. We've all gone our separate ways in the media, but still stay in touch. I'll have supper with Sebastian (whose company ended up being my agent), or Sharon (now a top music program producer) will come and stay with me in Yorkshire. The experience of making that program, forging a new style of television, brought us very close to each other. But we don't do group reunions—they are horrible beyond belief.

I attended architectural college in London and last year my contemporaries staged a reunion lunch. I walked into the room and thought: "Who the f*** are all these dreary old men?" Never again! Out of the ninety-five men and five girls I spent my college time with, I see just two on a regular basis and they are among my dearest friends. Forget the rest!

As for Friends Reunited—meeting up with those girls who made you feel thoroughly inferior at school because you didn't sprout tits when they did is my idea of hell. Those vile bitches called me a "lezzie" because I was six foot tall and had no chance of snaring a boyfriend to make out with at the youth club. They're only going to judge you again if your house is not as swanky as theirs, if you're not married, if you haven't got "gifted" kids and a nice car. F*** OFF!

AS FOR THE IDEA OF RE-DISCOVERING SOME BLOKE YOU FANCIED WHEN YOU WERE SIXTEEN—GET REAL!

TIME CAN CHANGE OTHER RELATIONSHIPS IN A POSITIVE WAY, THOUGH.

My younger sister died in 2006 after a horrible battle with cancer, and throughout our time growing up together, sharing a bedroom until we were fourteen and twelve, we were not particularly close. Our parents, who had a very troubled relationship, ran the household on a "divide and rule" basis. Consequently, my father had great ambitions for me. As a young electrician he'd studied at night school and had eventually qualified as an engineer. He wanted me to follow in his footsteps and nagged me constantly about studying and homework. My sister deliberately failed her exams and left high school as soon as possible—she felt second best. It was only after both parents had died that my sister and I could become friends. And when she died, I realized just what extraordinary people skills she had. Over sixty mourners packed into the chapel, all paying tribute to her as a special friend. Pat's manner, just like mine, could be brusque. She certainly didn't mince her words, and if you crossed her, you certainly knew it. But, if you were her mate, it was a different story. She loved going on outings with her mates, playing cards at lunchtime, going out for a drink, putting together bus trips to pop concerts. I miss her very much, but from her death I learned a lot more about how to run my life.

PAT'S DEATH HAS REINFORCED MY PRIORITIES—FRIENDS MUST ALWAYS BE THE BACKBONE OF YOUR LIFE.

Here's something I wrote about friendship in my column in The Independent on Sunday *in 2006—and it's truer now than ever:*

"Remember when you had real friends and not just the ones on the TV? We might mourn the demise of successful television series like This Life, Sex and the City, *and* Friends—*in which groups of thirty-somethings sat on sofas endlessly agonizing about life, relationships, and getting laid—but the truth is that those iconic programs represent a gorgeously seductive fantasy world. The reality for us, the viewers, is that all the demands of our daily lives mean that we have fewer friends now than ever before. Bosom buddies—the people you ask for advice and phone up when you're feeling suicidal, the people you are never going to have to have sex with—will soon be like rare breeds: something to be carefully protected and nurtured. Researchers have uncovered the depressing statistic that the number of people we confide our closest secrets and our intimate problems to has dropped by a third in twenty years. Even more worrying, a quarter of the men and women they spoke to admitted they had absolutely no one they could discuss the really important things in their lives with. How sad is that? We are becoming a nation of lonely, loveless singletons—and with text messaging, e-mails, speed dating, and*

voicemail, it's so easy to airbrush someone out of your life if they don't live up to expectations, or start proving troublesome. The end result is that we end up not just desperate and dateless, but friendless, too. Twenty years ago, people came home from the office and went to clubs. They did evening classes, or signed up for activities with co-workers. Now, traveling to work is stressful, and we end up devoting more of our lives to our careers than ever before. We might grab something to eat on the way home, fall into bed, or watch a DVD. The next day, and the next, we repeat the cycle. The success of online chatrooms means you can have intimate conversations with complete strangers and adopt any personality you like. No one is judging that midriff bulge, those double chins, your disastrous hair color, or those chewed fingernails. In cyberspace, you can be perfect. Real friends hardly exist. Intimacy is a frightening concept to an increasing number of people. The boom in text messaging—more impersonal than a phone call (in which your tone of voice and your mood can be judged and found wanting)—reveals just how disconnected we've become. It's important that we start to rediscover and put the effort into nurturing real friends—time-consuming and irritating as they may be—because, if we don't, we face a bleak and cheerless old age."

Back from the jungle and still being blunt

Tough at the top

LIFE'S

TOO

F***ING SHORT

TO SPEND IT

IN THE SAME

DREARY JOB

'I've proved them all wrong'

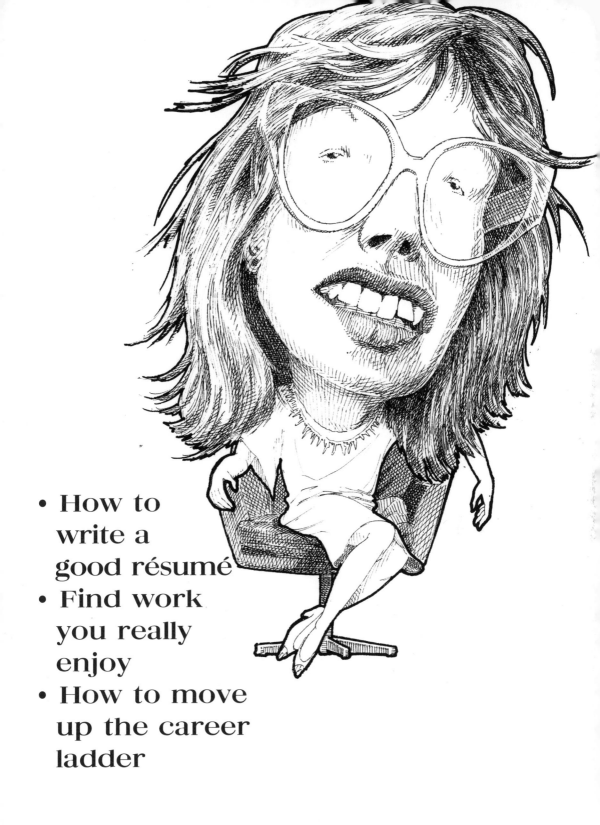

- How to write a good résumé
- Find work you really enjoy
- How to move up the career ladder

LONDON COUNTY COUNCIL

NAME

SCHOOL

We spend more than half of our lives at work · and so that time had better be good.

I have had a fantastic career. Correction: I am still having a great career. I have no intention of retiring, working less, sitting back, and letting others take my place. But I've had no children—consequently I've been able to concentrate all my efforts on achieving my goals. Planning a career is almost impossible for so many women. We have to multitask, work five times f***ing harder than any bloke to crawl up the greasy pole of success in the workplace, and combine all that with sustaining a relationship, keeping a family together, and running a home. It's our right not just to go out to work, but also to maximize our earnings, hold down a challenging and rewarding job, and build a career doing something that we enjoy. I can write that, you can read it, but we both know that the reality is that…

A2

LADY MARGARET SCHOOL

REPORT Name _Janet Bull._

Term _Autumn 1958._ Form _I7_ Average Age of Form _11.4_

Grades	Marks	Subject	Comment	
B.		SCRIPTURE	Good oral work, & usually good homework but Janet must learn with care.	Be
		ENGLISH	Really good. Janet works well.	M
+		GEOGRAPHY	Janet works well and with enthusiasm.	E.t
-		HISTORY ...	Janet shows enthusiasm in class but her written work is too often spoilt by carelessness	
		LATIN		
C		FRENCH—WRITTEN ..	Janet must always give her full attention in class and do her written work carefully.	
		ORAL ...	Her pronunciation is quite good.	C.N.
		ARITHMETIC		
B		ALGEBRA ...	Janet's work is usually good, but she needs to work more accurately.	
		GEOMETRY ...		E
B+		SCIENCE	Good. Janet works with enthusiasm.	Bn
B		ART	Good.	Jl
B+		~~CRAFT~~ WRITING ...	Good. Janet's writing is clear and attractive.	W.
C+		MUSIC	Janet is working well.	D.
		INSTRUMENTAL MUSIC	Janet has made a very good start.	E.C.
B+		HOUSECRAFT	Good. Janet works very well.	E.a.
		PHYSICAL EDUCATION	Good. Janet has worked well.	M.
		DANCING		

General Progress and Conduct:-

Janet is always enthusiastic and she must see that this pleasing trait is always allied to accurate work.

Times Absent _—_

Time Late _—_

Next Term _Jan 6._ to _March 25._

Half Term Holiday _Feb. 16 + 17._

Form Mistress _M.B. Jasaroou._

Head Mistress _F.E. Marshall_

Parent's Signature _PWG Bull._

WHAT WE WANT and **WHAT WE HAVE TO SETTLE FOR** are two depressingly different things. So let's get back to basics and see if there is any way you can improve your own situation.

I didn't always study hard in high school—instead I was undisciplined, always in trouble with teachers. But I worked in the public library in the evenings, read a lot, kept lists of films I saw, kept catalogs from all the art exhibitions I'd been to, filed the programs from plays I'd seen. In other words, I was a relentless self-improver. And it all paid off. School was a f***ing drag. I have always loathed rules of any description and the syllabus in subjects like history was mind-numbingly dull, but at least I passed enough exams to get into college to study to be an architect. And I prepared a portfolio for my entrance examination with drawings and photographs I'd taken of buildings that inspired me. I could talk about my interest in art and literature—by eighteen I knew what I liked and what turned me on creatively.

After a couple of years I realized that college wasn't for me—I would never be as good an architect as my close friend Piers—and so I decided to turn to my other great love, writing. I collected some sample articles I'd worked on, book reviews and opinion pieces that I'd written on spec, and sent them to half a dozen editors (of magazines I enjoyed reading) looking for work. I was lucky enough to land an interview and then a job on a weekly teen magazine, and within six months had been headhunted and taken on as deputy fashion editor by the *Daily Mail* newspaper. Within a year I was a columnist—at twenty-one! That just wouldn't happen today. There are simply too many people chasing too few jobs in the media. Nowadays I tell women to stay on at university for as long as they can, not to waste their time getting a degree in media studies, but to hone their brain by coming to grips with serious stuff like politics, history, or English. Degrees in geography are completely pointless, too, if you want to work as a writer or researcher.

HOW TO CREATE A GOOD RÉSUMÉ

What will get your job application noticed is not just a well-typed résumé, but lists of interests and activities you can add to it. People who spend time doing challenging things show adaptability and dedication that employers will always notice. Extra skills like computer proficiency and languages also play well. And be prepared to take a job working as an assistant to someone you admire in order to get a toehold in an industry or business you want to succeed in. My former assistants have risen to become drama and comedy producers, full-time writers, or directors of interior design firms. If they were smart enough and thick-skinned enough to cope with the stress of working with me, then they can run anything. Some went back to university and took degrees in Arts Business administration so they could run theaters or opera companies.

If you can't take the time to study full-time, why not do a degree at night or take classses online? It's never too late to get extra qualifications or to change your career. It doesn't matter if you are fifteen or fifty-eight, you owe it to yourself to keep putting stuff in your brain, otherwise you will turn into a boring, small-minded, elderly person—someone who feels that life has dealt them a short straw, someone who always harps on about the f***ing past. To everyone reading this book I say: it's the future that is the most exciting thing that's ever going to happen to you—not some snog behind the bike sheds when you were fourteen. What you are capable of achieving is limitless, and masses of input from a whole heap of sources and people is what will keep you youthful.

Let's sort out your résumé. **FIRST OF ALL, LEAVE OFF YOUR AGE—WHOSE F***ING BUSINESS IS IT ANYWAY?** You're going to be an asset to any organization no matter how old you are—that has to be your attitude. Discrimination by age is illegal, so if you

Sun Aug 19. Returned from Spain, arrived
9.0 at Perivale. Slept all morning.

Mon 20. Went to work - felt lousy

Sat 25 Edd, Joan, & I went up to Fair at Putney

Friday 1st Went to stay with Edd.

Sat 2nd Sept Phoned up mum - G.C.E results -
I passed both (howzat!) Went to
Pauline's party.

Sun 3. Sept Came home. Mum & dad gone
to Worthing. Joan came round.
Went to Lyons club - invented new
dance !!!!

Friday 7 Sept Card from Hugo. Finished
work. Wrote to Hugo.

Sat 8 Sept Started work in Chemist - it's
not very hard. Went to Roumph's
party.

Mon 10 Sept Another card from Hugo!
Hadn't posted letter so I just added
a bit on the end of it. Says he's
sending me a matelot shirt.

Tuesday 11 Sept Returned to school —
(Lousy) back to work now.

are asked your age at an interview, just ask why they want to know, or if you've not got the nerve to do that, just lie. Who cares? Leave your kids and your divorces off your résumé, too. That's of no concern to your future employer. Or your current marital status. Instead of listing your paltry qualifications at the top of the page, try enthusing about all your skills first. List your interests, your hobbies, how you spend your time outside work. Sound like you'll be a multitalented asset, not someone who is going to start moaning about how long it takes to get to work each day.

SHOW AN INTEREST IN THE COMPANY YOU WANT TO WORK FOR—and explain why! You'd be amazed how many people

came for interviews with me at the BBC who admitted that they had never watched a single program that my department had made. Why the hell would I ever want them working for me? Out of the door immediately! I am also astonished by how many people say they "want to meet famous people." Get real. **I AM HERE TO TELL YOU THAT MOST FAMOUS PEOPLE ARE F°°°ING BORING.** Work is about work, not the remote possibility of shaking hands with a famous TV personality or Elton John.

I can spot the good assistants and gofers—the lowest of the low—on any program I've ever worked on. They will offer to do just that little bit extra every day, unasked, in order to get noticed. Paid a pittance, they are desperate to clamber up to the next rung of the ladder. Good ones don't just get the tea and coffee, they've researched where you're filming, where to get something to eat. They subtly ingratiate themselves by offering to pick up your train tickets. They ask what you're writing about and offer to do some online research for you during their lunch hour. They are the chosen few who will go far, no doubt about it.

Janet Street-Porter   Adrian George

I love résumés from people who've studied history at an evening class, worked on archaeology projects during their vacation time, put in time at a local radio station, or volunteered to help out in a hospital or nursing home. I am interested in people who perform music, go to concerts, help young people, and pass on their skills to others. I am not interested in anyone who lists "meeting people," "eating out," or "traveling." You've always got to add that extra ingredient to stand out from the crowd.

If the worst comes to the worst, why not just lie about your academic qualifications? They are pretty meaningless anyway. I can't even remember my exact high-school examination results—does it really make one bit of difference? I did pretty well at high school, but I've met people with much better high-school grades than mine who wouldn't know how to run a small takeout restaurant and I've run multimillion-dollar businesses. My own mother (who was a highly intelligent, if somewhat difficult, woman) lied in order to get a coveted job as a clerical assistant in the civil service. She just said that she'd passed her exams at sixteen, when in fact she'd had to leave school at fourteen to work as a domestic servant for a rich family miles from home because her father had died, leaving her mother with a large family to bring up. Luckily no one ever bothered to check up on her—and to be honest, in thirty years I have never called up a school to check a job applicant's real academic qualifications either.

DECIDING WHAT JOB YOU WANT

Don't waste your time and money on these charlatans called life coaches— what a laugh! They call you up, charge you hundreds of dollars to tell you where you're going wrong and why you're depressed.

IT'S COMMON SENSE.

What books do you read? What films do you like?
What TV programs do you find engrossing?
Do you like meeting other people, or are you a loner?
Do you like teamwork?
Could you work from home?

It's not surprising that women, not men, start most of the new businesses in Britain

—even though it will mean spending five times the amount of time working, and definitely involve huge financial risk. Women want to work differently, set their own hours, and get away from the rigid hierarchies of male-dominated businesses, which involve time-wasting meetings and an overemphasis on routine and structures—pyramids of power with middle-aged blokes generally sitting at the top! But before you consider starting your own business, you've got to work for someone else to understand the competition and the marketplace.

I have been employed by big organizations like the BBC, run large departments, and also spent years working as a freelancer, writing from home and working for small television production companies. So I have experience with both ways of working. The most seductive but brain-numbing aspect of work is routine. My motto was never to stay in the same job for more than a couple of years—especially when I started out.

ACCEPT THAT YOU MAY BE FIRED OR MADE REDUNDANT

as companies downsize or reassess their priorities. It's not the end of the f***ing world! Just use it as an opportunity to try something different, and don't spend weeks being depressed and ruminating on the negative aspects of being laid off. It wasn't personal—you have to repeat and repeat and repeat that to yourself over and over again. Every time I have been dumped I have used it to my advantage—I left the *Daily Mail* when it downsized from broadsheet to tabloid format—and had already lined up a job at the *Evening Standard*. I got fired from Live TV, a small, new media venture owned by a newspaper group that had zero experience in broadcasting, after I made a speech about the M people—male, mediocre, middle-aged, middle class—who run television. I certainly didn't take it

personally. In fact, I was thoroughly relieved not to
have to trek down to Canary Wharf every day and
argue why topless darts and rugby (on a channel
set up to provide news and gossip) was a bad idea.

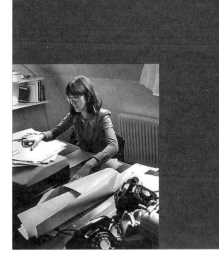

I have developed more than one set of skills, so
that if there's no work as a television or radio host,
I can earn money writing newspaper columns or
magazine articles. I can deliver speeches, present
awards, and chair public debates. I never wake up
and think my life is boring. I have constructed it so that I never have to do
the same thing for too long.

THE MOST IMPORTANT SINGLE QUALITY YOU NEED IS BELIEF IN YOURSELF.
Listen: I don't have a university degree,
I didn't study Classics, I have never been on a f***ing management course
in my life, but I have run departments of 350 people, edited a national
newspaper, and been a high-powered media executive. In the early part of
my career I never did just one job at a time—I worked as a radio host in
the mornings, and edited a magazine in the afternoons. In my spare time I
put together art exhibitions and helped out on new magazines. I wrote for
the glossies, for airline magazines, and for newspapers.

I never thought I couldn't do something. Be prepared to fail and learn from your failures.

MAXIMIZING YOUR
OPPORTUNITIES AT WORK

WHEN YOU START WORK, MAKE SURE YOU GET THERE EARLY. WEAR NONTHREATENING CLOTHES—THIS MAY SOUND AS IF I'M DESERTING THE SISTERHOOD, BUT I CAN'T STAND PEOPLE WHO TURN UP FOR WORK LOOKING AS IF THEY ARE GOING TO A PARTY LATER AND THIS IS JUST THE BORING PLACE THEY'VE GOT TO SPEND TIME AT BEFOREHAND. FOCUS ON YOUR RESPONSIBILITIES—START EACH DAY WITH A LIST OF WHAT YOU FEEL YOU NEED TO ACHIEVE, AND AIM TO COMPLETE ALMOST ALL OF IT BEFORE YOU LEAVE.

It's important to come across as someone with a sense of humor. You don't want to be considered a snob, but **DO NOT GET SIDETRACKED.** I loathe office gossip and have never gone out to lunch with anyone I worked with—I can't see the point. If I want a different background at lunchtime, then I take a newspaper and go and sit somewhere quiet, by myself. I do not want to be pals with co-workers.

REMEMBER: LIFE'S TOO F***ING SHORT TO SPEND TIME IN A JOB THAT'S NOT WORTHY OF YOU. YOU ARE ON A JOURNEY AND THIS IS JUST ONE STAGE OF IT.

JUST REGARD YOUR CURRENT STATUS AS TEMPORARY, ANOTHER STOPPING POINT ON YOUR ROUTE. READ AN INTELLIGENT NEWSPAPER EVERY DAY, THINK ABOUT POLITICS AND HOW THEY IMPACT ON YOU. DON'T OPT OUT OF LIFE.

Target someone at work you can do better than, and make sure that your bosses notice you by offering to take on all sorts of extra stuff outside your immediate job description. When I went to the BBC as Head of Youth Programmes, I didn't even have an office to start with! I had to spend the first two weeks camping out in a library in the children's department. I spent all my time watching as much BBC TV output as possible and carefully noting who were the wafflers and time wasters at management meetings where each week's programs were discussed by key executives. The bottom line was that the only way I could build up my department was by taking over airtime run by other people. For me to make programs, other executives had to have their programs canceled—of course they were not going to like it, but did I give a f***? I ruthlessly targeted certain slots, came up with dozens of options for every idea that was requested from my bosses who ran BBC 1 and BBC 2, and within two years I had 200 people working for me and my department had been expanded to include a whole range of feature programs, even though a Features Department already existed within the company—I never let that fact hold me back.

> Get up an hour earlier in summer and use that time to plan your day, to do something you want to do, either exercise, more walking, or making a list of priorities.

BE WILLING, BE COMMITTED TO YOUR EMPLOYERS, DON'T EVER BAD-MOUTH THEM WHILE YOU'RE ON THE PAYROLL, AND OFFER TO TAKE ON EXTRA STUFF LIKE COMMITTEES AND SO ON. BECOME NOTICED.

I was asked to join the so-called "Equality" Committee when I first joined the BBC—it had been set up to make sure that women and ethnic minorities got promoted. I thought it a complete waste of time and said I was sorry but I regarded signing up for an equality agenda a backward step. In my book I already belonged to the superior sex! I never bothered to get involved in anything specifically to do with women—a complete waste of time. We must not be treated as a special category if we are to compete and succeed in the workplace. Never ask for a favor at work—you'll be singled out as difficult if you do it on a regular basis. When people come and ask you to take on a task,

NEVER SAY THE FOLLOWING:

I'm already too busy.

I am not qualified to do that.

It's not part of my job description.

ALL OF THESE REPLIES MARK YOU AS A "NO" PERSON, WHEN THE WAY TO GET ON AT WORK IS TO BE A "YES" PERSON, WHO SAYS "OK, I'LL DO MY BEST."

There is no comeback to that. It is the perfect answer, because even if you fail in some small way, you have at least tried and shown that you are willing. I once had Darryl, a brilliant manager working with me at the BBC, helping to run around $60 million worth of programs a year. If I ever wanted to develop another project or come up with a costing to pitch for a new series, he never said "That's not a good idea," but always came up with the reply "OK, I'll work something out, let's go for it!"

If I was a bimbo I would not be running a TV company worth £30m

PLAN EACH MONTH, NOT EACH DECADE'

I never think about what I am going to be doing in ten years, five years, two years, or even next year. I work on the principle that the current job must be what I want to do until a better idea comes into my head. If I plan a project for the future and it doesn't get accepted, I plan out the amount of time I am going to spend trying to get it going and that won't be more than two months. Then, I file it and move on to something else. You can waste a lot of time and energy trying to sell ideas that there's no market for. Keep them—you can come back to them later—but move on. If you don't get that job you wanted, try another approach with someone else. It's extremely important to be flexible.

FINALLY:
LIFE'S TOO F***ING SHORT TO LISTEN TO OTHER PEOPLE'S CRITICISMS

Remember you are special. Never let any boss or any colleague try to make you feel otherwise.

IGNORE THEM. If I'd read all the shit that's been said about me, I would have done myself in by now. When I was offered the job of editing *The Independent on Sunday* newspaper you would not have believed the crap that other journalists—particularly in papers like *The Daily Telegraph*—wrote about me. Andrew Neil even asked me on the radio why I was qualified for the job! By the way, I had worked as a journalist for thirty years by then, but I hadn't gone through some dreary training scheme, hadn't worked as a news reporter, hadn't spent time working on a local paper. They wanted to imply that I was picked because I was well known! As if a newspaper proprietor is going to put a multimillion-dollar business in the hands of a halfwit. I had run large teams of people in television for decades. I had produced live programs that were two hours long, with a news agenda. I had won TV awards. But because I wasn't in their horrible little club, I was obviously crap. I had even presented the same political program as Andrew for BBC TV for two years, a fact he chose to ignore. The *Telegraph* hatred was more mysterious as I had regularly written for the paper in the past, until I remembered that the man who edited the *IOS* before me—who was fired—was married to an assistant editor at the *Telegraph*, so she was wreaking some kind of revenge. SAD COW.

MORAL:

Rise above your enemies, because you are bound to make plenty as you go through your working life!

← rook shit

I am sitting in Finh River Camp the bloody birds have already crapped on my shoulder! So that's 2 lots of good luck in 2 hrs!

You could see the concrete base & dirt road near our camp site. It a 5hr drive on dirt roads from Alice Springs. Two men had dam the river by making a concrete de & a pipe from it supplied the cha with water. Now the waterhole h silted up & the water was much lo the the dam, but it was a pretty impressive piece of work (abou 40 ft across & 20 ft deep) all sone. Now we walked down the mile s & the head west we a series of foothills

Lots of birds - dives diamad

we wal at & had c

Left margin:
of TS pat
boughne
nta,
tereture
cls and
not a
v for
6 of
d in the
river
, on a
Park.
ree
erigass)
p.
undy.

t up
r. Tidie!

camp
track
—

Serpentine
see
ed
is —

LIFE'S TOO F***ING SHORT TO WASTE MONEY GOING TO A SPA

- Forget going on a retreat
- Feed your mind
- Hang out with the locals

We go on vacations for all sorts of reasons—and radically changing the way you look should not be one of them. Let's be honest: ninety-nine percent of us definitely think our stomach is too fat, we don't like the dimply bit at the top of our legs, and we have permanent bags under our eyes that no amount of makeup can disguise. We could all do with a bit of improvement—but at what personal cost? When I work, I work f***ing hard, and so the notion of imposing some health routine on my vacation is ludicrous.

SPAS, in my experience, are places you want to **AVOID LIKE THE PLAGUE.** They are full of cash-rich, imagination-poor people being miserable together. You are never going to meet a single interesting person to shag or become pals with in a spa. I have wealthy friends who go to these places to lose weight—to be tortured—or to do a load of work. Sure they might lose five pounds, but within two weeks their weight is back to what it was before. Spas don't work in the long term—you have to change your life for yourself, not rely on some idiot in a white nylon overall who drones on about your chakras while rubbing oil into your hair and messing it up for weeks afterward.

Ask yourself: What do I want out of a mini-break? You won't get a smaller ass in five days, but you might sleep better and feel more relaxed if you adopt my set of rules and try a different, more realistic approach. My vacation mantra is:

WORK HARD AT HAVING AN ENJOYABLE AND REWARDING BREAK FROM ROUTINE.

That means creating your own agenda—more about that in a minute.

Remember, this is the modern world—you are not a monk or a nun. Ignore all the New Age drivel about rejuvenating your mind—it's just the latest rubbish beauty editors spout to make us feel insecure and spend money on pointless alternative therapies they got for nothing.

Once, we Brits went on something called a "summer holiday"—then it became year-round "mini-breaks." Now, we are considered vulgar and shallow unless we've booked something called a "retreat" where we pay a lot of money to have what has become known as a "therapy vacation." Notice how the word "holiday" in Britain has become a badge of vulgarity. Holidays are what "common" people do, people who go on all-inclusive package-deal trips, people who are happy to spend their time prone on a sun-drenched beach, reading paperbacks, slathered in lotion.

The single reason most people use for taking time off work in the twenty-first century is "stress." Stress did not exist as a sickness until the 1990s. For the previous decade lower-back pain was the single biggest reason used to take time off work. Please understand that providing relaxation is an industry like any other, and vacation operators have been quick to cash in on what they see as a wonderful opportunity to cater for our new-found stress, by coming up with experts who design time off for high-powered men and women who won't feel fulfilled unless they have spent a load of money on a "therapy vacation." These new versions of our old friend, the summer holiday, cost thousands of dollars and involve new-fangled experts called life coaches who sit and listen to you moaning on about what's lacking in your world and then come up with suggestions about changes in your career or living arrangements.

These "food for the mind" breaks have been a natural development from the self-improvement vacations where you learned to cook, meditate, went walking, or did art classes—all of which have loads of benefits. But I feel queasy at the idea of someone I have never met before stepping in and reorganizing my life.

For God's sake—there are far cheaper and better ways of dealing with a sense of grievance about how your life is shaping up!

Over 200,000 people in Britain went on what have become known as "wellness" vacations in 2006—and they are set to become even more popular. You need to have a long, careful think about the fantasy that you are signing up for: a couple of weeks in a ludicrous tropical setting, a house on stilts over water, plinky plunky bells every time you get hot oil dribbled on your "third eye" by an Ayurvedic masseur in a thatched palm hut. When you return home, there's only one way you're going to feel a week later—thoroughly miserable—when the lapping waves have been replaced by the drone of traffic, and the smell of incense replaced by the stink of your sweaty fellow commuters on the subway.

The big mistake about a wellness or therapy vacation is thinking that it will change your life in the long term. They are just an expensive bit of adhesive tape and don't imagine anything different. Psychotherapists agree that changing your location may make you feel better in the short term, but in the long term it will not have dealt with any underlying things that made you experience a sense of unhappiness or unease in the first place. It's like being on a TV reality show—but you are paying a fortune to participate!

At the end of a couple of weeks of massage and chats with therapists you will never see again, you've got to get on a plane, deal with the chaos at the airport, and return to the real world of a regular job, irritating kids, and partners who don't live up to expectations. And how do you know that the so-called experts you have bared your soul to are any good? The truth is, we are starting to use vacations to deal with our inability to sort out our priorities in life for ourselves, and that is really stupid. If you want to kick-start some changes, like eating differently, exercising, making new friends, and perhaps changing your job, a vacation can help by giving you the breathing space you need. But behavioral changes you start on vacation will be very hard to keep up when you return, and you could end up feeling even more dissatisfied than before. A week's worth of life-coaching with a therapist in the Maldives or Bali could cost you well over $6,000. But wouldn't you be

(Guadeloupe)

better off having a different kind of break and setting aside money for regular classes or activities when you get home, something that will have continuity and be an event you will look forward to every week through the dark days of winter?

I have been on every kind of vacation, from a luxurious retreat on a desert island to walking with a guide high up in the Dolomites. I have written about travel for thirty years. I've slept on the floor of public huts for hikers in New Zealand, camped in the Australian desert, danced with natives in a remote part of Papua New Guinea, and I've sailed on the same boat that the Queen chose for a trip around the Western Isles of Scotland. I've slept on king-size mattresses and on tatami mats in Japan. I've had mud baths and every kind of massage on every continent, and I've climbed Mount Kilimanjaro, the highest peak in Africa, and the Himalayas. I've had altitude sickness in Chile and wandered through the Blue Mountains in Jamaica accompanied by a guide called Sweet Pea. You can trust me—I've had some unbelievably shitty experiences along the way, but also some quite unforgettable ones.

But I use every trip as a chance to put something into my head—forget therapy vacations. Every journey I make, no matter how small, is something I regard as a plus.

RULE NUMBER ONE Never expect too much from a vacation. It will have good moments, boring ones, and unforgettable ones, all mixed up. It won't all be fabulous. I always TAKE A SMALL NOTEBOOK and in it I write my daily diary. It will contain complaints, joys, great meals, snippy remarks about my fellow travelers, comments about the weather, descriptions of sights, plants, birds, and number of insect bites sustained! I have kept all my travel diaries going back thirty-five years, and they make hilarious reading when

I get back home. They are a way of transferring any of the crossness or discontent I might feel about how the rest of my life is going onto the page, and replacing it with positive experiences to do with the place I am visiting. I cannot emphasize enough how keeping a record of your trip will make it live on afterward. I have diaries of all the long walks I've done, of weeks spent seeing churches and eating pasta in Italy, recipes for cake from Grenada, cocktails from New York, great thrift stores in Los Angeles, the names of trees in the forests of Tasmania. I have notebooks stuffed with postcards, tickets from museums I visited, and bus and train timetables.

RULE NUMBER TWO Decide that you will do ONE THING EVERY DAY THAT WILL BE MEMORABLE and put stuff back into your head. It might be a walk of up to two hours. It might be driving to see a church, a museum, or a park that you have never been to before. It might be taking the bus or train to visit another town or village for lunch. IT WILL NOT BE SHOPPING OR LYING DOWN READING A BOOK. Plan to do one thing each day that offers real input—it doesn't have to take ages. It is not just having a meal in your hotel. It is not just going for a swim or indulging in a manicure. Before you go to bed each night, plan your next day. Make sure you go on vacation with maps and walking guides. If you don't want to carry heavy books, just rip out the chapters that relate to where you are and carry those—guidebooks aren't sacrosanct volumes, like the Bible! It's really important to arrive at your vacation destination with as much information as possible and to get local walking maps from a tourist information center or your hotel as soon as you arrive.

C'mon in the WATER'S FINE

RULE NUMBER THREE

Your companion for this important break is not necessarily the person you have sex with. It is a big mistake to take more than one vacation a year with a partner you live with. Vacations are not shag-fests. Who wants to have sex when the beds are too narrow, the mattresses too hard, the walls too thin, and the air conditioning either freezing or useless? After a couple of days in the sun, you'll be covered in sore red patches and mosquito bites, not exactly conducive to wild sex! Vacations are about switching off, not settling scores. They are not an opportunity to start moaning about your partner's appetite, his fat gut, or her refusal to wear the clothes you want. Gay men make perfect vacation companions. They are not interested in your sex life, your fat midriff, or your cellulite—they've got the same issues themselves.

If you are going with a girlfriend, choose one who is not competitive in any way. If you like a glass of wine with lunch, then for God's sake don't choose a vacation companion who doesn't drink, or who counts units. Choose someone who likes silence when walking, who will let you read by yourself for hours on end, someone who will give you big chunks of the day to yourself, not some needy individual who feels the urge to compulsively fill every hour of the day with mindless gossip or chatter. Don't ever choose anyone in a different fitness league to you. When I want to go for a walk for a couple of hours a day, that's exactly what I am going to do—just a leisurely stroll, not a f***ing death march or speed walking. I am never on vacation to tone my muscles—I have a gym back home for that. Vacations are for toning the mind.

And don't on any account, no matter how much you are tempted, shag anyone you meet while traveling. See how they look back under the cloudy skies of home ground. And when you return, tanned, refreshed, and fit, maybe sex with your partner will be a little more interesting, you never know...

RULE NUMBER FOUR Forget everything fashion editors tell you about what to wear. How much do you want to look like a typical woman on vacation? No, I thought not. And don't ever believe the crap written about "minimal" packing. It's not something I've ever been able to achieve. It's a concept dreamed up by stick-thin females who'd look good dressed in a celery wrapper. My only advice is never to waste your money buying new clothes for a vacation— they are only going to get ruined with suntan lotion, insect repellent, pasta sauce, and red wine! Or the hotel laundry will shrink them out of all recognition, or press your favorite wrinkly linen frock into a stiff board.

Never buy a new vacation swimsuit before lunch, either. Go and try one on after you've eaten a couple of sandwiches—at least you know that it will fit in the afternoons. I don't know anyone who's actually ever lost weight on vacation, do you? Vacations, unless you have ignored my previous advice and have perversely opted to be punished in a spa, are for eating great food, drinking every day, and indulging yourself. I loathe all wrap-around dresses, wrap skirts, sarongs, and things that tie together. All these garments are bound to come undone in a breeze, and are guaranteed to make the wearer look like a badly packed sausage or over-stuffed parcel. The "wrap" concept only works if you have a waist and are a size 8— otherwise, I'm here to tell you, forget it.

What you and I need are clothes that fit around our shoulders and arms, and then gently float away from all body parts below, so that while eating, lounging, or strolling we do not look like a series of tires waiting for their hubcaps to be fitted. For that reason, never buy white trousers, white skirts, or white crop pants. Take a deep breath and simply leave them on the hanger. White clothes are God's way of telling us we're mutton dressed as lamb, that we're embarrassingly past it. White clothes were invented so the tabloid press could print pictures of well-known women on vacation looking like total trollops in their resort wear. Ditto high-heeled glittery sandals festooned with coins, jewels, and fringes. Having a lot happening on your feet is never going to detract from your shortcomings elsewhere, and you'll just look like a waitress serving beers in a pub.

RULE NUMBER FIVE Please do not opt for a destination that no one you know has ever been to, because you will have no barometer about what it's really like and where it's good to stay unless you have a particularly good travel agent, or a well-researched, up-to-date guidebook.

And if you have bravely decided (as I have on several occasions) to go on a trekking vacation that involves sleeping under canvas,

MAKE SURE YOU ARE PAYING FOR SOME OTHER F***ER TO PUT UP THE TENT AND DO THE COOKING!

I love camping, as long as I am bolstering the local economy by paying for a guide, someone to put up my tent, someone to bring me a bowl of hot water for morning ablutions, and a couple of people to rustle up gorgeous campfire meals in the evenings. Don't make the mistake, and completely false economy, of thinking you can do it yourself. Are you mad? Money spent like this is guilt-free. You are employing the locals, you are eating local cuisine, and your money is going directly back into the area you are visiting. I hate all-inclusive resort vacations with a passion. They contribute nothing to the neighborhood, they are surrounded by high walls and security guards. I will never give one dollar to any of them.

I have hiked all over Europe, New Zealand, and Australia, and I love staying in family-owned hotels, where they make me picnic lunches, where the rooms are basic but clean, and the setting is glorious. These are the experiences I remember and cherish, not the nights in luxury hotels full of tight-assed foreigners overdressed for dinner.

Traveling is the best present you can give yourself—and it's better than any drug, believe me.

carnet de VOYAGES

N

E

O

S

1991

AUTOUR DU MONDE
EN 80 PAGES

LOG OF THE JOURNEY continued

Date	Section	N.G.R.	S	C	A	D	Weather
Sun 24	Marrick Priory	SE 067978	2	108½	11.15		SUNNY!
	✓ Marrick	SE 076982	3	109½	11.45	12.00	and wind fe
	✓ Marske	NZ 105007	5½	112	12.35		lunch by bec
	Whitcliffe Wood	NZ 145014	8½	115	2.30		1-2
BANK MON 25 HOLIDAY	X Richmond	NZ 171009	10½	117	3.00	9.15	SUNNY
	✓ Colburn	SE 196991	3	120	10.15	10.20	SUNNY
	X Catterick Bridge	SE 228993	5½	122½	11.10	11.15	
	✓ Bolton-on-Swale	SE 251992	7½	124½	11.50	11.55	CLOUDY
	✓ Rawcar Bridge	SE 299988	11¼	128¼	12.55	1.0	
	✓ Streetlam	SE 310989	12¼	129¼	1.05	1.10	
	✓ Danby Wiske	SE 337986	14	131	1.35	2.45	NICE PUB
	X Oaktree Hill	SE 361888	16	133	3.20	3.25	getting colc
	✓ Long Lane	SE 389998	18½	135½	4.10	4.15	CLOUDY
	✓ East Harlsey road	NZ 418010	20½	137½			
	X A.19 road A19 TONTINE INN	NZ 442012	22½	139½			
TUES 26	X Ingleby Cross	NZ 449007	23	140	6.00	11.30	VERY COLD , GREY.
	Beacon Hill	SE 460998	2½	142½	12.40		HURRICAN
	✓ Huthwaite Green	NZ 492008	5½	145½		2.00	CHARLIE
	✓ Carlton Bank	NZ 522030	8¼	148¼	2.45		
	X Clay Bank Top	NZ 572033	12¼	152¼	—		
WED 27	Urra Moor	NZ 595016	2	154¼	12.10		HEAVY RA
	Bloworth Crossing	NZ 616015	3½	155¾	12.40		+ WIND
	✓ Lion Inn, Blakey	SE 679997	9	161¼	1.15	2.30	
	✓ White Cross	NZ 682020	10¾	163		10.00	
	✓ Glaisdale (station)	NZ 783056	18¾	171	6.00	9.45	Grey Sunny per iod
THURS 28	✓ Egton Bridge	NZ 804052	2	173	10.40	—	
	✓ Grosmont	NZ 829052	3½	174½	11.15	11.40	shopped in railw sho
	X A.169 road	NZ 862047	6	177	12.30		SUNNY!
	✓ Little Beck	NZ 879049	7¼	178¼	1.00		
	Falling Foss	NZ 888035	8½	179½	1.40	2.30	lunch stop
	✓ May Beck (car park)	NZ 892024	9½	180½			Clouded ove
	✓ B.1416 road	NZ 901041	10¾	181¾	2.55		
	X Hawsker	NZ 928074	14¾	185¾	4.10		
	X Robin Hood's Bay	NZ 953049	19	190	5.30		the sun cam out just as w went paddli

RULE NUMBER SIX Always explore a city on foot. From Mumbai to Santiago, Venice to Vienna, I always take a really good walking map and explore the city slowly on foot, stopping for drinks and lunch in small cafés. Hire a local guide or take taxis, if necessary. But never take an air-conditioned limo or a bus tour. I like the messiness, the noise and the cacophony of cities, the smells, the colors, and the shops. You will experience nothing but a blast of air conditioning in the back of a limo. So be brave. **LIFE'S TOO SHORT NOT TO HANG OUT WITH THE LOCALS.**

Years ago, I created a television series for the BBC called *Rough Guides*. The whole intention was to reveal the "real" version of great destinations of the world, from Senegal to Madrid to Jamaica to Naples. We asked local researchers to show us the hottest bars, the best small restaurants where they liked to eat, the most amusing clubs, and the unmissable shops. The series was a huge hit, shown all around the world, won loads of awards, was much copied, and ran for years. Let those principles guide how you travel in the twenty-first century.

DO WHAT THE LOCALS DO AND YOU WON'T GO FAR WRONG!

LIFE'S TOO F***ING SHORT TO LET SOMEONE TELL YOU HOW TO DESIGN YOUR HOME

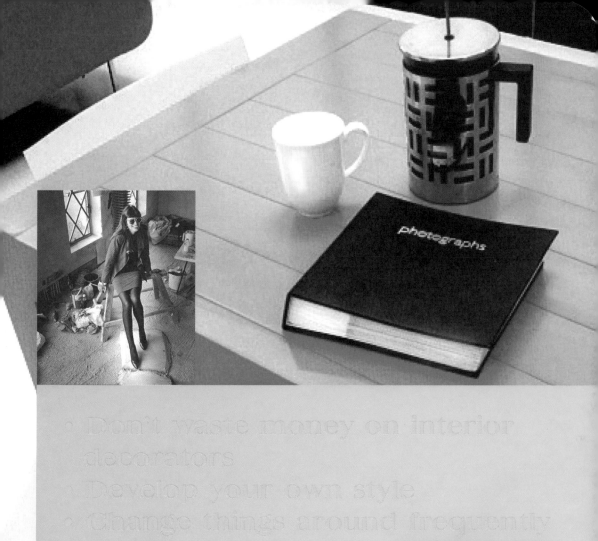

- Don't waste money on interior decorators
- Develop your own style
- Change things around frequently

I promise you, you don't need pots of money to realize your personal decorating style. The starting point is a strong belief that if you are happy in your surroundings you will benefit in all sorts of ways. What you categorically don't need is an expert, who will charge you well over $100 an hour, to do any of this. Forget it.

YOU DON'T NEED
* an interior decorator
* a big wad of money
* to spend hours poring over color charts

YOU DO NEED
* to have the guts to define your own style
* to edit your belongings ruthlessly
* to be prepared to spend time realizing your dreams

Over the years I have been pilloried, emulated, consulted, and paid a lot of money to talk about design. I have lived in one room in a shared apartment, a public-housing apartment house, a Georgian sea captain's house on the Thames, a tiny cottage in Yorkshire, and have been through the trials and tribulations of building a brand new architect-designed house in central London.

I AM NEVER HAPPIER THAN WHEN I'M REDECORATING, AND THE MINUTE MY PLACE IS FINISHED I START ALL OVER AGAIN.

I love shutting the front door and wandering around my home with music blaring. It's like starring in my own movie without the inconvenience of having a director, cameraman, or leading man.

Let's start with the most important room: the one where you sleep. What do you want to look at before you crash out at night? Clutter or simplicity? I look at endless magazine articles about other people's houses—they always look so tidy, so organized, so unlike my own. I make sure I have the biggest cupboards or storage space I can get, with doors that close completely—forget window shades or curtains. Then I edit my clothes to fit that space, and store everything else in boxes or chuck it away if I haven't worn it for two years.

KEEP IT MOVING
THROUGHOUT MY LIFE I HAVE HAD A TERRIBLE TENDENCY TO COLLECT:

art deco furniture, paper fans from the 1920s, teapots, Susie Cooper and Keith Murray pottery from the 1940s. I went to flea markets all over Britain and the Continent for twenty years. (At one stage I was married to a man who had the same affliction—he'd amassed 1,000 pieces of blue-and-white Staffordshire pottery, 200 bully beef can openers, a collection of swords, and military watercolors. Nightmare!)

COLLECTING ON THIS SCALE IS A DRUG—DON'T LET IT TAKE OVER YOUR LIFE.

By the time it got to be 1986 I had so much stuff it filled three storage units, where it gathered dust while I built a brand new house. It had to go. I sold my designer clothes from the 1960s–1980s at auction houses and flea markets. I did a load of flea-market sales with my sister. I ran a couple of celebrity rummage sales and sold all the art deco furniture back to the antique dealers. I purged myself of the need to collect on this scale ever again. The husband went, and so did about seventy-five percent of my stuff. I kept a few pieces of china, and I display them on an old dresser where nothing matches. Nowadays, if I see I have got too much stuff building up, too many plates shaped like fish (I collected about a hundred), too many whimsical salt-and- pepper shakers, or too much junk jewelry, I pick out my favorite six or seven pieces and get a friend to sell the rest for me on eBay and we split the profit.

Life's too short to think this stuff is going to go up in value. Sell it and be grateful for whatever you get.

"EDIT, EDIT, EDIT"

The longer you look at most collectables or ephemera, the more you take them for granted, whether they are paintings, prints, vases, or pebbles you found on a distant beach. Change the objects on your mantelpiece or bookshelves every few months, and you will be surprised how much you'll like the new display. Look at the stuff on your walls and re-hang it every couple of years. Take those crappy posters to a rummage sale.

WHAT'S THE BIG DEAL ABOUT HAVING A WALL FULL OF DUSTY PAPERBACKS?

Do you have so little self-esteem you want visitors to be impressed by your feeble library? Go through every book you own and only keep the ones you loved so much you might read them again, the ones that someone special gave you, the reference books, or the ones that are truly beautiful. You can take the rest to a charity thrift store or a secondhand book shop. Books that just sit doing bugger-all fill up space, which is expensive to rent or buy and could be used more productively.

must be your mantra.

NEVER GET SOMEONE ELSE TO
DESIGN YOUR HOME

Browse through magazines and you'll soon realize you can put together a personal style by ripping off ideas and color schemes, but not by wasting large sums of money on furniture and curtains. As for hiring a kitchen designer—why bother? You can go to IKEA and pick their brains for free; most stores have kitchen planners now. Most architects (in my experience) are useless at designing kitchens that work properly.

When it comes to structural changes—like taking out walls to open up space, putting in new windows, or building an extension to add light to your kitchen—find a local architect and look at their work to see if it turns you on. Ask if they have a junior member of staff who will come to your home and make suggestions about opening up existing space or using it more efficiently. But pre-set a fee, and don't agree to pay them a percentage of the final costs of any rebuilding. Talk over your ideas, look at their suggestions, and then run the job yourself. It's the only way to cut costs and keep things moving.

I like my surroundings to be a mixture of the old and the new. I loathe interiors that are all of the same period—they date quicker than any dress or coat.

I put pictures of friends in frames I've collected from rummage sales and flea markets or bought new. I change them every year, and keep rearranging them. I collect odd jugs, pots I've picked up on my travels, funny old menus, handmade walking sticks. I mix the cheap with the rare. I don't let any one kind of object dominate. I found some old embroidered samplers and had them framed, along with drawings collected over the years, masks from around the world.

The key thing to remember when decorating is to keep the overall look as simple as possible.

In London I have a white living room, and to complement this dazzling brightness a metal garden table was sprayed shocking pink to make a great dining table. The chairs are the basic plastic stackable variety, with striped cotton cushions (meant for outdoor lounger chairs) from France to make them more comfortable. The color scheme is restricted to bright acid primaries, with a turquoise sofa and homemade cushions covered with jazzy cotton remnants found at a street market. This look was very cheap to create, accentuated with weird light fixtures (one made from a cactus that I carried back from the States) and the minimum of clutter. When I get bored with it, the sofa (currently covered in electric turquoise tweed) will be recovered or sold at an auction house.

I have had four different sofas in the last eight years. It's important to treat them like fashionable frocks—they are the central feature of the room and you will get bored with them.

I'VE CERTAINLY CHANGED SOFAS AS OFTEN AS I'VE CHANGED MEN. SOFAS ALWAYS ACCOMMODATE MY BIG ASS WITHOUT ANSWERING BACK. A good sofa is the most important piece of furniture after your bed. A sofa is where you weep when you're lonely, slob out when you're feeling sick, and get down and dirty when you're in that all-too-brief hot stage in a new relationship.

FURNITURE IS THERE TO DO A JOB—IT'S NOT YOUR BEST FRIEND, SO WHEN YOU GET FED UP WITH IT, SELL IT AND MOVE ON.

My style is not easy to pin down. Rubbish and good art are all given equal importance. The main criteria is that my odds and ends all mean something to me. They are not there to impress anyone else, and that's the best advice I can give you.

HAVE THE GUTS TO PUT YOUR FAVORITE THINGS AROUND YOU, NOT SOME SOULLESS FABRICATED LOOK DREAMED UP BY AN INTERIORS MAGAZINE.

I don't care if stripped pine is "in" or "out." I buy old chests of drawers or desks and drop sinks into them for my bathrooms—that way I get a set of drawers for makeup and towels underneath. I got rid of curtains in my Yorkshire farmhouse and had wooden folding shutters made. The old pine floors were stripped and waxed and covered with rag rugs made in the 1950s that I bought in local junk shops. In the corner is a funny little table my dad made from bits of a telegraph pole during the war. I've got an art deco vase full of shocking pink fabric roses from Woolworths adding a splash of color to a dark space.

A couple of years ago the *Sun* newspaper found out that I had a tiny house on the sea in Kent. They turned up when I wasn't there and managed to see inside and told their readers that my main decorating crime was painting the walls magnolia!!! The idea that the f***ing *Sun* is some sort of arbiter of style when it comes to interiors is so funny, isn't it?

Personally, I have always thought that there's nothing wrong with painting your walls cream

—what I can't stand are snobby cows who drone on about how they've chosen really expensive latex paints based on heritage colors, with a tiny hint of blue or yellow in the white, manufactured to an ancient formula by a really expensive paint company.

Ninety-nine people out of a hundred cannot tell the difference between ordinary white and designer-white paint.

Same with creamy "linen" drapes. I used metal scaffolding poles and bought the cheapest unbleached cotton I could find to make drapes for my beach house. The bed was made from recycled wooden railroad ties by a carpenter friend, and I covered it with old cotton quilts. I buy cheap wool throws when I am driving through the Scottish border country, in blue and white checks and stripes that fit in with my color scheme. It's not exactly rocket science.

The stackable dining chairs are unpainted galvanized steel, the dining table made from ribbed aluminum.

THE TRICK IS TO LIMIT THE RANGE OF COLORS AND MATERIALS

—loads of shades of blue, a basic creamy white background, and different gray metals for furniture and lighting. All as simple as possible.

I would not dream of telling you how to decorate, I can only tell you how I do things—

you have to have the guts to realize that there's no right or wrong way to personalize your space. The key thing is to express yourself.

IN BRIEF

* Cut out clutter.
* Choose a color palette that is appropriate for a light or dark space, one major color and a complementary one (e.g., cream and blue for a light space, hot mustard and rich burgundy for a dark one).
* Group your small objects together, and change them.
* Chuck out your furniture or move it around every couple of years.
* Mix old and new, junk-shop finds and special things.

LIFE'S TOO F***ING SHORT TO BE A SLAVE TO FASHION

- How to make your body look its best
- Finding bargains
- Putting together your own look

SAY IT AFTER ME: I WILL NEVER BE SEEN DEAD IN

* a poncho
* wedge-heeled shoes
* PVC trousers
* a jumpsuit

NO NO NO!

Personal style has to be something you feel very comfortable with. Forget what anyone else says. I have always had a very strong idea of how I wanted to dress. The *Daily Mail* once ran a double-page spread of things I'd worn over the past twenty years—obviously there were some horrific outfits, but at least I looked unmistakeable! In Britain we have the most diverse, creative, and imaginative population in the world—look at our fashion, our art, our contemporary music. Celebrate whatever rich mix you are a part of and express yourself.

WHAT YOU WEAR SHOULD NOT BE A SOURCE OF PAIN, VAST EXPENSE, OR MISERY. LIFE'S TOO SHORT FOR ALL OF THAT, AS THIS BOOK KEEPS TELLING YOU. THE MOST IMPORTANT THING IS TO UNDERSTAND WHAT WORKS FOR YOU AND STICK TO IT. IGNORE WHAT THE FASHIONISTAS DICTATE.

How depressing it is to see women everywhere cramming their feet into revolting wedge shoes because fashion editors have decreed they are the "latest" look. There is never going to be a right time for certain items of clothing, no matter what these self-appointed gurus might say.

STITCH AND BITCH. From the age of eleven I was obsessed with clothes and learned how to sew by adapting patterns so that they became what I thought was stylish. I kept a notebook in which I detailed everything I made and how much the fabric cost. I saved up for things I really wanted, like a leather jacket, and then rolled it up and slept with it under the mattress for two weeks so that it didn't look embarrassingly new on its first outing. That was what being a "mod" meant—it was like a religion. Certain things had to be perfect, like heavy shoes, long, narrow pencil skirts, and handbags lined in suede.

In my twenties I spent four years writing about fashion for the *Daily Mail* and the London *Evening Standard*, attending all the couture and ready-to-wear shows in Paris and London. Never again! That intensive period of being immersed in the lunatic world of high fashion turned me off it, and most revealingly, I discovered:

Many of the people who write about and photograph fashion have nothing but contempt for ordinary people.

They are not interested in your personal problems. They exist on Planet Fashion, where they truly think that next season's color or heel height is more important than poverty, mortgage rates, or teenage drinking. I used to think all that mania was entertaining. Now it just seems obscene and quite irrelevant.

Clothes 1963	cost	paid for by
5. Jan. Handbag.	1 - 10 - 0	me.
26 Jan. Navy jumper	1 - 10 - 0	25/- me 5/- mum
7 Feb. Coat	10 - 10 - 0	mum & dad
23 Feb. Cardigan	2 - 7 - 6	£2-5 mum 2/6 me
23 Feb. Brooch	Given	by mum.
4 March Blouse	1 - 14 - 11	mum
30 March Denim Jeans	1 - 10 - 0	£1-5 me 5 mum & da
Scarf	Given	Aunty Eileen
17 April Shoes	3 - 0 - 0	Mum
5 May Scarf	-	Nain
11 May Nightie	-	Mum
25 May Dress Material etc.	1 - 10 - 0	Me
8 June " "	1 - 5 - 0	Me
22 June Denim Skirt Brown	1 - 10 - 0	Me
22 June Tee Shirt	16 - 11	Mum
4 July Plimsoles	17 - 11	10ˢ Mum 8ˢ me
11 July Swimsuit	2 - 0 - 0	Mum
13 July Dress Material	1 - 1 - 0	6ˢ mum + me 15ˢ
20 July Bag	1 - 0 - 0	Mum
22 July Slip	10 - 11	Me
20 July Bra	7 - 6	Mum
23 Aug Flat Shoes	2 - 0 - 0	Me
23 Aug Suede Shoes	3 - 0 - 0	Me

In the twenty-first century the old idea of fashion having seasons is bonkers. You don't chuck out one load of clothes to replace them with a new look any more, but fashion editors still carry on with this antediluvian way of thinking. THE REASON IS THEY WANT US TO CONSUME MORE THAN WE NEED, to keep the business that pays their salaries ticking. Cheap clothes made in the Third World, often by workers who earn less than their national minimum wage, have flooded into Britain. Now we buy jeans for $20, T-shirts for $4, party dresses for $40, and chuck them out after a couple of wears. They generally look dreadful after they've been washed half a dozen times anyway.

This is a horrible way to dress. You wouldn't eat cheap, nasty muck that was produced in horrible conditions, so why wear it?

The items I'm most loyal to (worn over and over again) in my wardrobe are coats. I always laugh when I read fashion editors telling us to forget about coats, jackets are in. Don't they ever have to wait for a train in December? Don't they ever have to walk to the store in the wind? Don't they ever have to stand in a line outside a cinema? Unless you have a chauffeur, loads of cash for taxis, or a private jet, you'll never ever manage to get through the winter without a heavy coat. And don't think that wearing a padded ski jacket looks anything other than sad.

Around thirty years ago, Doug Hayward—the famous tailor who dressed people like Sean Connery and Michael Caine—made me a beautiful long, narrow, single-breasted navy blue cashmere overcoat. I still wear it, proof that a great coat never really goes out of style. I have early Alexander McQueen numbers in brown wool and black cashmere, and beautiful tweed coats by Dries Van Noten that are fifteen years old. I never buy cheap coats. I buy a new coat in a color or a fabric I haven't already got every couple of seasons. I still have a yellowy-green Max and Co silk summer coat from ten years ago and one in bright cobalt-blue suede by Betty Jackson that I picked up on sale. The only time I chuck out coats is when they fall to pieces, like the turquoise mohair Gucci trench coat that ended up looking like a matted doormat!

The right clothes should make you feel better—but, for most of us, shopping for something to wear is a horrible experience. Life's too f***ing short to patronize snooty designer boutiques.

A few years back I went into a famous boutique off Bond Street in London to buy a dress by Alexander McQueen that I'd seen in a magazine. A stick-thin snotty woman approached me and when I described the dress I was looking for, in a size 12, she gave me a pitying look—as if I had just wet myself—and came out with the following:

"I'M SORRY MADAM WE DON'T SELL THAT SIZE HERE!"

What planet are these cows on? The average woman's dress size in Great Britain is at least an American size 14—and by the way, most designer clothes are bought by women over thirty, and the majority of these customers are not size 6, 8, or 10 and never will be.

The best way to shop to avoid ritual humiliation is on the Internet or by using a personal shopper in a good department store. When you buy online, make sure you can exchange your purchases. Be honest about your size, and ask loads of questions about fit and cut. But don't ever get addicted to online high fashion—it won't get you a lover, a better job, a nicer home, or a friend. All it gets you is debt!

In-store personal shoppers don't charge for their services. I use the excellent team at Liberty in London. They know my size, what I like and don't like. It's always worth spending an hour explaining all this when you first meet. You can ask them to call you when something has come in that might suit you. You can phone or e-mail from wherever you are, and they are trained to solve your immediate problem—a dress for a wedding, a suit for an important interview. They don't force you to spend money you haven't got, they don't bully you, and they know who else has bought the dress you might be interested in. They are experts at working out how to disguise your fat ass, your nonexistent waist.

Every female executive I know uses a personal shopper. They are far more honest than any of your girlfriends.

Don't be intimidated. Every good department store has a personal shopping department and it's there to be used.

Buying clothes this way means you actually spend less, because you acquire single pieces that work well and last more than one year, like well-cut trousers or a tailored jacket, and then you can team them with basic T-shirts or skirts from a chain like Gap. I avoid small boutiques like the plague. If you are not a size 6, 8, or 10, they will not have your size in stock. They are too intimate, and it's hard not to get swept up into buying things because the sales assistant is raving about them. In a department store you can be more clinical and detached.

BUYING JEANS —ANOTHER ONE OF LIFE'S NIGHTMARE EXPERIENCES.

Jeans are another disaster area. We're offered so many different cuts—high-waisted, low-rise, boot-leg, narrow, flared, and wide. I feel anxious every time it's that time of year when I need to buy another pair of jeans. SOLUTION: I simply go into a department store with a large men's department, select the best-looking young male assistant, and tell him to choose a pair of jeans for me. I couldn't give a f*** what he thinks about the size of my ass. Believe me, there will be plenty of other fatties coming into this place in the course of any week, simply by the law of averages. Best to select a weekday morning, when the place is virtually empty and the staff are so bored out of their brains they will willingly search through every rack until they come up with your size, in the hope of scoring some commission. Better still, ask your gay male friends if they are chucking out any jeans or contemplating sending any to the thrift store, in which case you can make a charity donation in return for their castoffs. That way you get a great pair of designer jeans, already worn in, probably from a price range you would never have considered in the first place.

NO ONE IN THE FASHION BUSINESS EVER PAYS THE RETAIL PRICE FOR ANYTHING.

Ignore what fashion magazines decree is this season's look. Instead, try a limited version of it, either by choosing a color, a hot new fabric, a top, or a pair of opaque or patterned pantyhose. My basic wardrobe doesn't change much: men's jeans (longer, narrower), big cardigans in bold colors, white or black T-shirts from Loft (I pick them up when I am in Paris, but they have a website and also sell well-made basics like straight-leg long sweat pants); very few dresses, because they are not adaptable. The ones I do have are in soft jersey prints and do not crease when they are packed in my suitcase.

GO FOR CLASSY CLASSICS IF YOU WANT TO WEAR SHOES FOR MORE THAN THREE MONTHS.

I paid over $800 for a knockout pair of black biker boots by Versace six years ago, and I still wear them every single winter, so that's excellent value for money. I have black suede ankle boots by Tods from the 1980s, Y3 trainers in plum patent that are five years old, jeweled Ferragamo pumps that were a present a decade ago. I only wear flat shoes during the day, but then I am six feet tall and don't need to try and elongate my legs. High heels are strictly for parties.

FIND A GOOD DRESSMAKER

Ask everyone at work and where you live if they know someone who is good with a sewing machine. Some dry cleaners have very skilled people doing alterations. A good dressmaker will take your favorite trousers apart, and then remake them in any suitable fabric. Once you've got trousers that fit perfectly, all you need is a couple of pairs of jeans and then you're set. I have remade skirts from wrap style to zippered, turned them from long to short, made culottes into softly gathered skirts, and bought a Donna Karan suit in a sale with the jacket a size too big and turned it into a perfect autumn outfit for $20. Because I sewed all my own outfits as a teenager, and made clothes for boutiques when I was a student, I've realized that sewing is not a skill to be sneered at.

I have a wonderful dressmaker who has made me costumes for special events and unusual weddings. She's made me a jacket out of black feathers for a black tie ball, and a black halterneck dress suspended from a jeweled curtain ring. She's made little bra tops to go under sheer cotton blouses picked up for $10 in India, and lined baggy linen trousers so they'll drape instead of wrinkle.

Buy fabrics when you travel. I bring back lengths of silk, embroidered cotton, plain linen. I buy old curtains in flea markets, pieces of lace. I stockpile fabrics and one day they will be turned into something special by my dressmaker.

A designer dress isn't sacrosanct—it's only a bloody dress, not a religious relic for God's sake. I have had all my designer clothes altered after I've got tired of them—sleeves taken out, skirts shortened, dresses recut. I never bother worrying about what the designer might think. Clothes are there to serve me, not vice versa.

OPEN YOUR WARDROBE DOOR. CHUCK AWAY ANY CLOTHES YOU HAVE NOT WORN FOR TWO YEARS.

* Give them to cancer fundraisers.

* Give them to a charity store.

* Give to them your cleaning lady.

* Give them to thinner friends.

* Or have a clothing swap one evening with your friends, (crack open a couple of bottles of wine and swap all your unwanted clothes).

Don't hoard the unwearable, the unfashionable, and the unspeakable mistakes.

And remember,

Don't get me wrong—after all these years I still love reading about fashion. But I will not be a slave to it. I ruthlessly filter what I see. I decide only to adapt or adopt what is appropriate—

WORKING OUT WHAT SUITS YOU IS THE TOUGHEST CHALLENGE.

Reflect new trends, but don't invest in them heavily. Nothing will age you more quickly than looking like mutton dressed as lamb. Avoid clunky jewelry unless you are six foot tall. Cut out the extra layers, the trailing scarves, the flapping bags, the unnecessary frills. Think streamlined, no matter what the fashion editors say. When you find something that works on you, buy a couple of them.

FASHION IS EXHILARATING, ENERGIZING, FUN— IF YOU MAKE IT WORK FOR YOU.

If you allow it to dominate your life, or be a source of major anxiety, that's not right. When the clocks go back in the fall, pack all your summer clothes away for the winter—that way you get more wardrobe space. Take them out at Easter, and dispose of what doesn't fit or what looks unappealing!

LESS IS MORE.

LIFE'S TOO F***ING SHORT TO HAVE A SET OF RULES YOU CAN'T LIVE UP TO

* See through the twaddle in the media
* Make your own rules and stick to them
* Stop fretting about finding the best beach bag / bath oil / T-shirt

We're supposed to be cash rich and time poor. We in Britain have the mental burden of carrying considerable personal debt, some of the largest in Europe. In short, our credit card spending is out of control. We use shopping to make us feel better, but in the long term the debt ends up making us feel worse. But what makes me feel even queasier than a large credit card bill is too much choice. The byproduct of our affluence and our emotional and cultural poverty, the logical conclusion for a society in which shopping is now regarded as a legitimate pastime or hobby like fishing or judo, is that we are offered miles more choice about every aspect of our lives—as if that's somehow empowering us and reinforcing our individuality. Hey—I can spend a lot of time choosing from 100 different corkscrews, so I must be a highly intelligent, conscientious consumer! Utter garbage!

Too much choice is thoroughly debilitating and solves nothing. It just creates more problems—the main one of which is that exercising choice eats up valuable time, and for what?

CHOICE DOESN'T NECESSARILY MEAN YOU ARE CHOOSING BETTER QUALITY, OR THAT THE END RESULT WILL ENHANCE YOUR LIFE IN ANY WAY.

Of course, a basic level of choice is a good thing, as it allows us to buy everything from food to gadgets to clothes and even homes based on what we would like to spend and what our personal requirements are. But the level of choice that we are offered routinely by retailers whose only motive is more profit for their shareholders is repulsive. Take tomatoes, for example. You and I are bound to have the same basic criteria when we buy a tomato. We would like it to be ripened in the sun, full of flavor, and hopefully not sprayed with chemicals and pesticides. You could apply the same criteria to most fruit and vegetables and perhaps add the notion of buying stuff grown locally when possible, produce that's in season, stuff that's traveled as few air miles as possible, and is organic, if appropriate.

Much has been written over the last decade about how EU bureaucrats in Brussels have instituted so many rules and regulations that fruit and vegetable growers have abandoned cultivating loads of old varieties of apples, plums, and spuds. Every Sunday, newspapers like the *Telegraph* repeat the same old mantra. Curiously enough, the reverse has now happened, and many small organic farms grow lots of interesting vegetables, fueled by customers looking for something different. Supermarkets have leapt on the bandwagon, with the result that they now offer so many different varieties of tomatoes you feel almost faint with indecision. But the key criterion must always be—are any of these tomatoes delicious? Whether they are the size of marbles or tennis balls, plum shaped or round, hanging on a vine, yellow, maroon, striped green and orange, or blood red, what do they taste like?

Taste must be the primary consideration for buying food, unless you are a complete cretin.

Most supermarkets pack and transport their fresh (and I use that word loosely) produce miles away from the stores where it will be sold, so it is generally not picked at the peak of ripeness—consequently most of it is thoroughly tasteless. And once you have put a tomato, no matter what the variety, in a fridge, you have ruined its wonderful flavor permanently.

Think of happy red tomatoes as friends—they are going to brighten up your meal, so why shut the poor things in a chilly dark white plastic cabinet for the last few days of their lives? If God had wanted us to eat tomatoes that lived in fridges he wouldn't have created them growing from yellow flowers on large green leafy plants that thrive on just two things—water and hot sun—neither of which is found inside a refrigerator.

I used to love the smell of my grandfather's house in Southgate, North London, where he grew all his own vegetables and kept chickens and ducks in the backyard. The sideboard was packed with red and green and orange stripy tomatoes ripening in large bowls, squash marrow sat in wooden boxes on the kitchen floor, and there were jars of chutney under the stairs along with ranks of bottled plums ready for the winter. The smell was overpowering, heavy, and seductive. The smell of summer. Not a smell encountered in the aisles of our supermarkets.

And it's not just major supermarket chains that are guilty of giving us meaningless choice. Take Whole Foods. They dominate the American market and have built up a billion-dollar empire with the patronage of the health-conscious middle and upper-income consumer in major cities across the USA. Now they seek to do the same in Britain, opening a massive flagship store of 7,500 square meters on Kensington High Street in London, in the middle of the richest borough in Britain, a department store for the most discerning foodie. They offer shoppers a hundred kinds of olive oil, forty different kinds of bread, forty types of sausage, seventeen kinds of coffee bean, and over four hundred cheeses. Harrods with a conscience, if you like. Banks of cabbages and lettuces, sprayed to look ultra-fresh and glistening—the way you certainly won't be feeling after spending hours wandering up and down the aisles trying to decide what to buy. Twenty-one different kinds of tomato! Less than forty percent of the produce is organic, and it is sourced from all over the world, offering us

LIFE'S TOO SHORT FOR

what appears to be the pinnacle of choice—but what does that really mean? I'll tell you—it represents the death of the small retailer, the kind of place where an owner imposes their personal taste on the contents of the store and customers buy that knowledge.

I'd rather visit a shop where I am offered a couple of kinds of coffee, tasted and chosen by the person behind the counter. I want to buy bread that they have sourced, that they like eating. There's a little delicatessen on the main street in Whitstable, Kent, that does just that. It's tiny, only holds about three people, but the owners have chosen the cheese, they've sourced the olives. They have selected a few wines that complement their wares. They have wild boar pâté, delicious Spanish ham. Anything from this shop makes the basis of an instantly delicious supper. Sometimes there are baskets of vine tomatoes or slabs of focaccia, strewn with sea salt and rosemary. This is a shop where the owners eat what they sell. In towns and large villages in France, Italy, and Spain, these shops and stalls in weekly markets still exist.

Choice is a complete waste of time when it comes to food, unless that choice has been made by someone with impressive taste and a commitment to quality

—not an executive whose primary concern is meeting quotas and dealing with marketing initiatives coming from a central office, which could be hundreds of miles away. All over Britain small shops are struggling as we

THAT KIND OF CHOICE.

sign up to this mad notion of choice, opting to buy our food in vast supermarkets where convenience overrules any other consideration. And the irony is, we end up spending more money on food we won't eat, and buying stuff we don't need and won't use simply because it was offered to us.

Marks and Spencer in Britain is another case in point—how many bloody types of bread do they sell? It doesn't matter what they call it, M and S bread will never measure up to the bread produced by Betty's bakery in Yorkshire, where a Fitness loaf is packed full of nutritious seeds and feels chunky and heavy like an old-fashioned loaf, not a substitute for a bath sponge. The reason why people form a line every day outside branches of Betty's in York, Harrogate, Northallerton, and Ilkley is because they know that the bread they are going to purchase will taste like bread.

Choice is exhausting and a vastly overrated concept, and no more so than when you go into a clothes shop in search of what we might consider basic clothing.

Once, you could buy a plain white T-shirt at the Gap, with a round neck or V neck, with or without a pocket. It was a staple in many a vacation wardrobe, chucked away after a couple of years when it had gone gray or blue because you stuck it in the machine with jeans by mistake. Then, Gap decided to enthusiastically embrace the concept of "choice." Now we have stretchy T-shirts that cling to our bulging midriffs, we have thin T-shirts that we are supposed to buy several of in different colors and "layer," which for most women simply means drawing attention to the rolls of cellulite around your waist. Believe me, layering, like wrap dresses, is a concept best left to those under twenty. After that you look like a parcel that's coming undone or a war victim dressed by a relief agency.

WHEN YOU FIND A T-SHIRT THAT WORKS, BUY TEN. SAME FOR SIMPLE COTTON UNDERWEAR. IT CUTS OUT HOURS OF SHOPPING OVER THE COMING YEAR.

When my old undies and T-shirts go gray, I use them as dusters or rags to wash the car. I am not being miserly, just recycling.

THE BEST OF ANYTHING IS A RUBBISH CONCEPT

Every week, newspapers and magazines fill their pages with lists of "the best" gadgets, sofas, lampshades, compost makers, beach bags, and solar-powered lighting.

I flick through these articles and tear them out. But do I ever buy anything? Never. I worry about the taste of the journalists who wrote the piece. I worry that they made their choice based on a press release or an important advertiser or a freebie. Unless I know them personally, I simply don't believe what they say, and neither should you. All of it is simply geared to getting us to consume more—and that is surely a bad thing.

Life should be getting simpler, not more complicated, as we sift our way through these choices we never realized we had to make. How can there really be one mixing bowl that's better than another, one purse that's the "best" choice, or one set of dishtowels that is superior to all others? Get real—choice is a drug you have to kick.

LIFE'S TOO SHORT TO WASTE ENERGY ON THESE UNIMPORTANT SELECTIONS OF THINGS WE DON'T REALLY NEED.

Real choice can only be achieved by setting your priorities and sticking to them, from choosing a car to buying food, clothes, even a home. Don't be afraid to chuck out the notion of valuing choice—it doesn't mean you are behind the times, stuck in your ways, narrow minded, penny pinching, or thrifty. IT MEANS YOU ARE SUPER SMART. It's tough, and many people might sneer, but by eliminating excess choice, you immediately feel liberated from much of the dross of modern life. Stick to local shops, or the recommendations of people you know.

ONLY BUY WHAT YOU NEED FROM PEOPLE WHO HAVE SAMPLED OR USED WHAT YOU ARE BUYING.

Go on your instinct, not the wordy crap of some junior editor at a glossy magazine or newspaper filling space on a features page where an ad got canceled.

HOW CAN THERE BE A "BEST" BATH OIL? USE YOUR HEAD.

RULES, RULES, RULES

Along with a plethora of unnecessary choice, we are constantly being assaulted with "rules" to live our lives by, from what to eat, to how to shop, to ethical living. In this book I am begging you to set your own agenda, not to be dictated to by outside interests whose only concern is profits, not quality of life. This book isn't a manual with an agenda you can cut out and keep, a list of rules that will help organize, reshape, and improve your life in some unspecified mysterious way. No way! Once I left high school, I left the concept of rules behind. I am a person who has always loathed any figure of authority and rules of any kind, from my brief period in the Girl Guides, to my short-lived time as a monitor (never a prefect) at high school, to my stint as a sales assistant in Woolworths, and my hopeless couple of months as a trainee in the civil service.

I HATE RULES UNLESS THEY ARE OF MY OWN MAKING.

Every day we seem to be targeted by so-called "experts" telling us how to conduct our lives, and the most irritating are employed by the ultimate nanny state, the British Government. We have Health and Safety notices on footpaths, large ugly signs banning smoking in front of beautiful medieval churches. Walk by a river and there's a stupid sign telling you the water is cold—no, really?? We have directives telling us to eat five portions of fruit and vegetables a day for our well-being, and guidelines from the Department of Health stating that women should not drink more than fourteen units of alcohol a week and men twenty-one. None of these so-called "initiatives" has done a single thing to stop young people drinking and smoking too much, or the collective weight of the nation verging on that of a million jumbo jets. Time and again, rules dictated from afar don't work.

I care about global warming as much as the next person, but "ethical living" is monitored by rule-making busybodies.

First we were told to fly less, use the train more, to carbon-offset all our travel. Then we were told that tree planting is not the solution as trees can trap the wrong gasses, and then it turned out that some of the companies set up to run all these carbon-offsetting schemes were investing in projects that would never really make much impact. Confused? I certainly am. Remember when we were told plastic bags were eco-disasters, and one store after another said they would stop handing them out or charge for them? Then Sainsbury's had the "bright" idea of commissioning designer Anya Hindmarch to come up with a $10 canvas shopping bag, on the side of which was emblazoned the motto "Not a plastic bag." It sold out straightaway and then started to change hands on the Internet for up to $90! Then we discovered that Anya's bags had been made in factories in China where wages and working conditions left a great deal to be desired. So these so-called "ethical bags" turned out to have been made by poor workers in a country halfway around the world that's one of the planet's major polluters. No wonder people question every day if it's worth making a personal effort to live their lives by so-called green values, when so many businessmen are plainly exploiting the current focus on the environment by producing goods that (on the surface) seem to be "better" choices.

I look at a factory spewing out fumes in China, Russia, Eastern Europe, or Korea and then I walk down to the recycling bins clutching my reusable canvas bags full of newspapers, bottles, and cans, and wonder if I am really making any difference whatsoever, especially when there are plenty of arguments about the value of recycling. I take care to buy recycled toilet rolls and kitchen towels, but is using Kleenex a crime? If the hard-core eco-lobby had their way we'd all be using earth toilets and torn up old bits of newspaper, making compost with our food scraps, and installing wind turbines on the roof. But wind turbines aren't a solution on an individual scale—you can't store the electricity, and they can be an eyesore. Why not just use less power? And the massive wind farms being built off the coast around Britain have another problem no one in government wants to talk much about, and that is the building and location of the large processing plants for this power when it is brought onshore, often in remote coastal areas of outstanding natural beauty. To me, these reprocessing units are as repellent as nuclear power stations—and government ministers will make sure that any planning considerations or local objections will be overruled, all in the name of green energy.

DECIDING HOW TO LIVE IN AN ENVIRONMENTALLY FRIENDLY FASHION CREATES MORE QUESTIONS THAN IT EVER ANSWERS.

You could spend hours debating whether buying beans flown in from Kenya is a good or a bad thing. On the one hand, it's a lot of air miles, so bad for the ozone layer, and the beans won't exactly be fresh by the time they reach you, but on the other hand, your money is helping poor, rural families get educated and have food.

EVERY DAY, ONE SET OF RULES IS SUPERCEDED BY ANOTHER. NO WONDER WE ARE CONFUSED.

Remember when butter was bad for you, and low-fat spreads were all the rage? Then we were told light, easy-to-spread substitutes couldn't lower your cholesterol by themselves, and good old butter was back in fashion. Finally, the Mediterranean diet, with plenty of olive oil instead of butter, grilled fish, fresh vegetables, and red wine, was touted as the way to a longer life and less heart disease. But living the Mediterranean diet only works in the Mediterranean, where it has evolved by using seasonal, local ingredients. It's pretty silly to try and emulate this in Chicago or Edinburgh in December.

Rules are invented by public relations and marketing people anxious to promote their wares.

Ninety percent of all the so-called "scientific evidence" you read in the papers or hear about on radio and television comes from surveys that have been funded by special-interest groups—fruit growers who want you to eat more blueberries, vegetable farmers keen to sell cabbage and broccoli. We're told that Brussels sprouts cure cancer, raspberries help your heart, and oily fish makes you brainier. All comical if it were not for the fact that so many of us avidly read and believe these unreliable findings. There's a watchdog group called Sense About Science that was created by independent scientists and health professionals and not funded by the corporations they investigate and review. Visit their website www.senseaboutscience.org.uk.

www.senseaboutscience.org.uk.

THE "RULES" WITHIN THIS BOOK ARE SUGGESTIONS FOR WAYS YOU CAN SIMPLIFY YOUR LIFE—GOALS FOR YOU TO SET FOR YOURSELF, NOT EDICTS TO BE OBEYED AND IGNORE THE CONSEQUENCES.

Deciding how much time you are prepared to devote to shopping ethically, recycling, and running your home in an environmentally aware way is purely a matter for you alone.

THE MAIN THING TO REMEMBER IS NOT TO BE BULLIED, ESPECIALLY BY PEOPLE WHO ULTIMATELY ARE ONLY INTERESTED IN GETTING YOUR MONEY FIRST, AND SAVING THE PLANET SECOND.

MAKE YOUR OWN RULES—AND CHANGE THEM WHEN IT SUITS YOU.

We're not monks and nuns living in the Middle Ages—our lives must be enjoyable and contain pleasure as well as work. Be clear about which ethical values and consumer choices make you feel comfortable—and you shouldn't feel guilty as a result.

FINALLY...

This book was written to make you feel good about yourself. Life should not be a series of tests that you fail to varying degrees, but a chance to celebrate your individuality. Above all, have a laugh…and thank God you don't have to live up to some ridiculous notion of perfection. Take a look at your favorite celebrities (like Victoria Beckham)—do they really look happy?

Life's too f***ing short to be on a permanent diet, worried about whether your clothes have been approved by the style police, and whether you're clutching the latest designer bag.

TAKE CHARGE OF YOUR AGENDA AND CUT OUT THE CRAP. GOOD LUCK.